THE ANTITRUST PENALTIES

THE ANTITRUST PENALTIES: A STUDY IN LAW AND ECONOMICS

KENNETH G. ELZINGA AND WILLIAM BREIT

NEW HAVEN AND LONDON, YALE UNIVERSITY PRESS, 1976

Library of Congress catalog card number: 75–43316
International standard book number: 0–300–01999–8

Designed by Sally Sullivan
and set in Times Roman type.
Printed in the United States of America by
The Murray Printing Company, Westford, Massachusetts

Published in Great Britain, Europe, Africa, and Asia (except Japan) by
Yale University Press, Ltd., London.
Distributed in Latin America by Kaiman & Polon, Inc., New York City;
in Australia and New Zealand by Book & Film Services, Artarmon, N.S.W.,
Australia; in Japan by John Weatherhill, Inc., Tokyo.

CONTENTS

ACKNOWLEDGMENTS

Chapter 5 and other short sections of this book were first published in a somewhat different form in the *Journal of Law & Economics,* vol. 17, no. 2, October 1974. In chapter 7 we have drawn upon our essay "Antitrust Penalties and Attitudes Toward Risk: An Economic Analysis," which was published in the *Harvard Law Review,* vol. 86, no. 4, February 1973. Some passages in chapter 1 and chapter 9 have appeared in *The Antitrust Dilemma,* edited by J. Dalton and S. Levin, Lexington, D. C. Heath, 1974, as well as in the *Emory Law Journal,* vol. 23, no. 4, Fall 1974.

We presented portions of this material to George J. Stigler's Workshop in Industrial Organization at the University of Chicago in May 1974. We are grateful to Professor Stigler and to the following participants in the workshop for their penetrating criticisms and helpful suggestions: Gary S. Becker, Kenneth W. Dam, Isaac Ehrlich, John P. Gould, Reuben Kessel, William Landes, B. Peter Pashigian, Sam Peltzman, Richard A. Posner, Melvin Reder, and Richard Zerbe.

Kenneth G. Elzinga used part of the material in this book in public lectures at various colleges and universities in the United States during the 1973–1974 academic year, when he was a Phi Beta Kappa Visiting Scholar. William Breit presented sections of the volume to seminars conducted at the University of Washington, Florida State University, and Louisiana State University. In a general way we have also used remarks delivered to the November 1973 American Bar Association Antitrust Section meetings in San Francisco. We are indebted to the many persons who helped us clarify our arguments during these pleasant and profitable jousts.

Earlier versions of parts of the manuscript were read and criticized by the following colleagues and friends: Gary S. Becker, Ward S. Bowman, Edgar K. Browning, James M. Buchanan, Kenneth W. Clarkson, W. P. Culbertson, Jr., Victor P. Goldberg, Thomas F. Hogarty, Richard A. Posner, Warren Schwartz, Roger Sherman, and Gordon Tullock. We owe them much for generously giving of their time and aid.

The authors gratefully acknowledge the Sesquicentennial Associate-ships granted by the Center for Advanced Studies at the University of Virginia which provided "research leave" enabling us to complete work on certain chapters of the book. In addition we wish to thank Ronald H. Coase for inviting Elzinga to be a Fellow in Law and Economics at the University of Chicago Law School during a most stimulating winter and spring of 1974.

Anyone who knows Walter Adams will recognize his influence on the choice of this topic. Truly it can be stated that this book would have been impossible without the model before us of his unremitting enthusiasm for the subject of antitrust.

Finally, we want to thank Judy Goertz, who performed yeoman's service as our research assistant, and June Morris, who patiently and with uncanny skill typed the manuscript.

INTRODUCTION

On December 21, 1974, President Gerald Ford signed into law the first major reform in the nation's antitrust laws in almost twenty years, which provided the most significant alterations in the penalties for antitrust violations since the enactment of the Sherman Act in 1890. In his economic message to Congress on October 8, 1974, the president had requested key changes in the antitrust penalties as part of his program to combat inflation. When finally passed a little over two months later, the Antitrust Procedures and Penalties Act changed violations of the Sherman Act from misdemeanors to felonies; increased the maximum jail term from one year to three years; and raised the maximum fines from $50,000 to $1 million for corporations and from $50,000 to $100,000 for individuals.

The new law was approved with astonishingly little dissent. In the Senate the bill passed by a vote of 92 to 0, and in the House a unanimous vote was recorded. This display of concord on an issue once so controversial is indicative of the wide-ranging consensus that now exists about the necessity of maintaining a high degree of competition in the American marketplace, a belief adhered to not only by politicians but also by civil servants, legal scholars, and academic economists. The importance of antitrust enforcement is one of those rare issues that cuts across even the most formidable of ideological barriers.

Yet there are different methods for approaching the study of antitrust reform. The first and most common is to study the general intentions and results of our institutional arrangements and, if it seems warranted, propose reforms. The antitrust literature has been almost wholly devoted to this approach. There is by now a whole spate of books and articles concerned with such questions as: Do concentrated market structures yield monopoly power? Do tying contracts enhance or diminish economic efficiency? Did Judge Learned Hand stifle legitimate business expansion in the *Alcoa* decision? Does the price discrimination law have pro- or anticompetitive implications? Basically all of these inquiries have in common one issue: what are the anticompetitive implications of various business practices? Once the answer to this question has been determined, a rational criterion will have been established to direct enforcement officials in the selection of antitrust cases. While we do not deny the importance of having better benchmarks by which to appraise the appropriate choice of antitrust cases, the chapters that follow will have little to add to this literature.

The alternative approach we pursue accepts the general structure of present legal arrangements and studies whether or not the methods and instruments of their implementation are efficient. This route seems particularly attractive after the substantial refurbishing of our antitrust instruments that has recently occurred. It seems likely that a long period of quiescence will now set in to allow a testing period for the updated weapons of antitrust. After all, the new legislation, although enacted swiftly in response to the urgent appeal in the president's economic message at the end of 1974, followed two decades of discussion before congressional committees and debates on the floor of Congress, during which there were no fundamental alterations in the penalties for antitrust violations. Because it is highly probable that there will now be a hiatus in legislation involving these penalties, an economic analysis of the inventory in the entire antitrust arsenal, both of the old and tested weapons and the newer deterrents, seems both timely and sensible.

Therefore we are not here concerned with the question of whether, for example, a particular tying arrangement or merger lessens competition. Our focus is on the efficient deterrence of antitrust violations—however these violations may be defined. And since deterrence is a function of the penalties imposed on violators, our analysis takes the form of a technical examination of the weapons that comprise the antitrust arsenal. The most rational criteria by which antitrust cases might be selected are useless if the violation is neither deterred nor remedied, an example perhaps of what Justice Jackson meant in his cryptic comment about the government having "won a lawsuit and lost a cause." It is curious that students of antitrust should be almost wholly preoccupied with the first approach virtually to the total neglect of the second.

Regardless of the approach taken, any proposal for reforming our antitrust arrangements must ultimately be based on a theory of government action. Should government be concerned with the achievement of competition and how much antitrust activity should be undertaken to bring it about? Chapter 1 provides a rationale for antitrust intervention in the marketplace and attempts to establish the limits beyond which such activity should not be carried.

We are persuaded that a legal and economic analysis of the deterrence issue in antitrust cannot be undertaken without an understanding of the historical context of the antitrust penalties. Since previous experience with these tools is the only evidence available for predicting the relative merits of alternative arrangements, chapters 2 and 3 discuss these instruments and place them within the setting of the American experience. In particular, chapter 3 surveys the public action penalties of incarceration, structural relief, and fines. Both the current status of these penalties and proposed alterations in their design are described and evaluated.

In chapters 4 and 5 the celebrated second barrel of the antitrust shotgun, treble damage suits, comes under scrutiny. First the historical background of reparations-induced, multiple damage actions is adumbrated. Then a thoroughgoing examination of the economic implications of the treble damage penalty is undertaken. Our use of the economic theory of property rights leads to conclusions that will seem surprising and new, we believe, even to specialists.

Chapter 6 tackles the question of trust-busting itself by examining the economic considerations of dissolving ongoing firms. Here too our treatment is rather unconventional, especially when compared to the portrayal of this instrument typically found in the antitrust literature.

Of necessity the longest chapter in the book is devoted to what we consider to be the efficient approach to antitrust enforcement. Chapter 7 begins with a discussion of the reciprocal nature of the monopoly problem. We analyze the psychology and incentives of corporate managers as they consider engaging in antitrust violations and show the crucial bearing that managerial risk attitudes have on the efficacy of alternative penalties in deterring anticompetitive activity. The chapter ends with a proposal for streamlining the tools of antitrust enforcement.

In chapter 8 we compare the relative merits of public versus private use of the antitrust weapons. The vehicle for this discussion is a series of questions that must be faced by anyone proposing sweeping change from a private action approach to sole reliance on public enforcement. Chapter 9 provides a statement of our conclusions.

PART I: THE SETTING

1

ANTITRUST AS A PUBLIC GOOD

Monopoly as Market Failure

The orthodox rationale for the antitrust laws is that they promote competition and prevent "undue limitations on competitive conditions."[1] From the point of view of economic analysis, however, public policy to promote competition can be explained as an attempt to come to grips with "market failure." Market failure occurs when voluntary exchanges do not sustain desirable activities or eliminate undesirable ones.[2] The spillover effects of production (or consumption) that are not taken into account through markets are called externalities and are usually associated with "public goods."

The two distinguishing features of a public good are indivisibility and nonexcludability. Indivisibility means that the consumption of the good by one person does not diminish the possibility of its consumption by another as well; that is, a public good permits simultaneous consumption. Nonexcludability means that once an indivisible good is provided, it is not possible economically to exclude others from its enjoyment.

National defense is a traditional example of a pure public good. Not only is it indivisible since one person's consumption of its services does not preclude others; it is also nonexcludable since it is not economical to prevent the enjoyment of this service by excluding those who refuse to pay for it.

1. U.S., Justice Department, Attorney General's National Committee to Study the Antitrust Laws, *Report,* at 1 (1955).
2. For a technical discussion of market failure, see Francis M. Bator, "The Anatomy of Market Failure," *Quarterly Journal of Economics* 72 (August 1958): 351; reprinted in William Breit and Harold M. Hochman, *Readings in Microeconomics,* 2d ed. rev. (New York: Holt, Rinehart, and Winston, 1971), p. 518.

Whenever a public good as just defined exists, it is unlikely that the optimal amount of it will be provided privately, because individuals have an incentive to behave strategically, dissembling their preferences in the hopes that others will provide the service. Since everyone has an incentive to "free ride," not enough public goods will be provided through a system of voluntary exchanges and market failure will occur. In such cases, government provision of the good or service is given consideration. Market failure has become the central explanation or justification for much government activity.

When seen in this setting, the antitrust penalties are simply an attempt to provide a public good, although the problem is not conventionally handled this way in the literature. Milton Friedman, for example, gives two *different* justifications for government intervention: (1) the existence of public goods and (2) monopoly.[3] But that is a distinction without a difference. In fact the elimination of monopoly is a public good in the purest sense. It is both indivisible and nonexcludable. One person's enjoyment of the services of a noncollusive market does not preclude others from that enjoyment; nor is it economical to exclude others. In other words, changes in market behavior affect all consumers simultaneously. It is not possible to have some consumers purchasing in a market with only a single producer while others purchase the same product in a market with many sellers.[4]

To illustrate, consider a simple case in which a firm that is operating in a perfectly competitive market enters into a collusive arrangement whereby it agrees with its former rivals to charge a higher price and to produce at a lower rate of output. Assuming that the cartel is successful, figure 1 illustrates the damage done to society by this individual firm. At competitive price P_0 the firm produces output Q_0, and the firm is economically efficient since the condition of efficiency is that price must equal marginal cost. After joining the cartel, the firm adjusts its output to

3. Milton Friedman, *Capitalism and Freedom* (Chicago: University of Chicago Press, 1962), p. 28.
4. It would not be advantageous for a monopolist to sell at marginal cost to some and not to others because those who buy at the lower price would sell to others at a higher price (but one lower than the price the monopolist would be charging). Moreover, under the antitrust laws such price discrimination might be illegal.

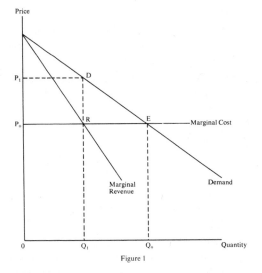

Figure 1

Q_1 and charges the price P_1, which is higher than marginal cost and violates the efficiency condition. The loss to consumers (called consumers' surplus)[5] is represented by the area of the trapezoid P_1DEP_0. Part of this loss, however, is a transfer of revenue to the cartel—the transfer being measured by the rectangle P_1DRP_0. This area must be subtracted from the trapezoid in order to get the net loss to society

5. Consumer's surplus is the difference between how much a consumer pays for a commodity and how much he would have been willing to pay rather than go without it. This surplus is an index of well-being. If it could be measured accurately, it would provide a test of the amount of welfare our economy generates for consumers. All that would be required is a list of the maximum prices a consumer would be willing to pay for each unit of a good, compared with the price he actually pays. In figure 1, consumer's surplus at price P_0 for Q_0 units of commodity X would be approximated by the triangular area CEP_0. This area is only an approximation to consumer's surplus unless it is assumed that the marginal utility of money is constant. It is assumed that such a small amount of money is spent on each commodity that changes in money's marginal utility can be ignored. Under this assumption the area under the demand curve and above the price line represents precisely the amount of consumer's surplus. On the more technical aspects of consumer's surplus, consult George J. Stigler, *The Theory of Price*, 3d ed. (New York: Macmillan, 1966), pp. 78–81.

caused by this individual member of the cartel. The net loss is represented by the area of the triangle DER. This is often referred to in the economics literature as the "welfare triangle" and is used to indicate the net loss to society from monopolistic behavior.[6]

Assume that the firms in the cartel are all alike, in the sense that they have identical cost curves and are of the same size. It is then possible to multiply the welfare triangle area by the number of firms to get the total loss to society from this particular price-fixing activity. If we could perform this calculation for every firm in the economy that is engaged in illegal monopolistic behavior, we would have a rough approximation of the total benefit to be gained from the elimination of monopoly power and the restoration of competition.

Note that in a world of no transactions or information costs (and one in which people did not attempt to act as free riders), the benefits of competitive markets would be readily secured. The customers of any monopolist would find it to their advantage to get together and bribe the monopolist to behave like a competitive firm, producing at an output where price is equal to marginal cost.[7] By so doing, the gain to consumers (in the form of increased consumers' surplus) would be larger than the firm's reduction in monopoly profits (and the amount of the bribe) and consequently (in principle) any monopolist could be com-

---

6. In this book, the primary goal of antitrust is taken to be allocative efficiency. There are, of course, other goals; for example, an equitable distribution of income and a rising growth rate. However, as Ward Bowman has pointed out, neither of these goals necessarily conflicts with the goal of economic efficiency and they can be achieved by more direct means (e.g., a progressive tax system combined with a negative income tax; programs encouraging savings and investment) than antitrust enforcement. For a fuller discussion of these issues, see Ward S. Bowman, *Patent and Antitrust Law: A Legal and Economic Appraisal* (Chicago and London: University of Chicago Press, 1973), pp. 5–14. Most economists now agree that the welfare triangle underestimates the actual loss in efficiency, because it does not take into account the investment of resources in the activity of monopolizing and in policing the cartel agreement. On this point, see Gordon Tullock, "The Welfare Costs of Tariffs, Monopolies, and Theft," *Western Economic Journal* 5 (September 1967): 224; and Harvey Leibenstein, "Allocative Efficiency vs. 'X-Efficiency,'" *American Economic Review* 56 (June 1966): 392.

7. It should be noted here that we are assuming a single price monopolist in the classical sense.

pensated sufficiently to induce him to forego monopolizing and to instead provide a greater supply of his product at lower prices. Both the monopolist and its customers could be made better off.

But one reason such behavior does not occur in the marketplace is the existence of an incentive for individuals to feign indifference to the possibility of having the monopolist produce where price equals marginal cost. Given the free rider problem, the establishment of competitive markets is a public good in the classical sense.

However, where there are significant costs of exchanging information between the parties actually damaged by the monopolist, and substantial negotiation costs as well, the free rider problem is compounded. For even in the unlikely case that all the customers of a monopolist shunned free riding (that is, everyone was willing to pay his share), the costs involved—assembling the potential customers, collecting their payments, and negotiating with the monopolist—could exceed the benefits derived from competitive behavior. In such a case, government intervention to provide the public good of competitive markets becomes explicable; the antitrust penalties can be seen as an attempt to eliminate the public bad of monopoly.

How Much Antitrust Enforcement Is Optimal?

Theorems on Antitrust Enforcement

It might seem that antitrust policy should be directed toward the elimination of all anticompetitive inefficiencies so that each and every welfare triangle could be captured for society. Economic theory, however, provides two traditional objections to the perfectly competitive model as a guide to public policy. One is the theory of "workable competition" proposed by J. M. Clark; the other is the theory of "second best" associated with J. E. Meade.[8]

8. J. M. Clark, "Toward a Concept of Workable Competition," *American Economic Review* 30 (June 1940): 241; reprinted in *Readings in the Social Control of Industry*, ed. E. M. Hoover and J. Dean (Philadelphia: Blakiston, 1942); J. E. Meade, *The Theory of International Policy* (London: Oxford University Press, 1955), vol. 2, *Trade and Welfare*.

Clark's theory held, in the first place, that if society's goal is socially desirable economic performance from some real world industry, it will probably not be attained by imposing or requiring all of the structural and behavioral conditions of perfect competition. For example, if some industry were characterized by substantial economies of scale, then imposing the perfectly competitive structural condition of many independent firms upon that industry would in fact lower its economic efficiency. Clark further reasoned that enforcing any *one* of the conditions of perfect competition in some industry where all of the conditions could not simultaneously be met could conceivably harm the economic performance of that industry. For example, if the exploitation of scale economies dictated the existence of only a few firms in a particular industry, then the imposition of the perfectly competitive condition of openly quoted prices could conceivably lower the industry's economic performance by serving to reduce competitive price cutting. Although Clark's theory today may seem to make an almost trivial point, at a time when economic theory and antitrust were struggling with the then new revelations regarding imperfect competition at the hands of Chamberlin and Robinson, his contribution was seminal and generated enormous comment.[9]

In contrast to the theory of workable competition, the theory of second best demonstrates that if one of the industries in an economy does not generate the optimum results of perfect competition, then the attainment of (or movement toward) perfect competition in other industries may actually lessen overall economic welfare. For example, if one industry in an economy continues to exercise market power (or incurs any effect, such as external economies, that causes its price to diverge from marginal cost), then efforts by society to attain the results of perfect competition in other sectors of the economy (through antitrust policy,

9. Clark's theory is not noted for precision, and its application is not without difficulties. Stephen Sosnick has surveyed the vagaries of much of the early literature of workable competition. See "A Critique of Concepts of Workable Competition," *Quarterly Journal of Economics* 72 (August 1958): 380. Proponents of strong antitrust enforcement feared that incorporation of the theory of workable competition into antitrust policy would provide a "cornucopia of escape hatches." See Walter Adams, "The 'Rule of Reason': Workable Competition or Workable Monopoly?" *Yale Law Journal* 63 (January 1954): 348.

regulation, taxation, or whatever) may be counterproductive and in fact lower the value of total output.[10]

Thus Clark, in an eclectic fashion, formulated a theory about optimality in particular industries: as a result of the characteristics of some industries, it may not be socially desirable to enforce all (or any) of the conditions of perfect competition in them. Later Meade fashioned another theory pertaining to overall economic optimality: if the results of perfect competition are not attained in some sector of the economy, policies that move society toward the results of perfect competition in other sectors of the economy may lower economic welfare.

It has not been explicitly recognized, however, that even if demand and supply conditions were amenable to all of the conditions of perfect competition, and even if "first best" solutions were attained in every sector of the economy, it would still be efficient to have a policy that stopped short of enforcing perfect competition. Indeed, in the general case, even if the Clark-Meade objections concerning movement to perfect competition did not apply, capturing all of the welfare triangles for society would be incorrect policy from the point of view of maximizing economic welfare. This rather paradoxical result is important enough to be expressed in the form of a theorem: *If a strictly laissez-faire policy does not bring about perfect competition in all markets, then it is incorrect economic policy to attempt to achieve perfect competition in the economy as a whole through antitrust enforcement.*

The reason the theorem has not been previously formulated is because economists, in their enthusiasm for the benefits to be derived from increasing competition, have lost sight of the not insignificant costs that antitrust enforcement imposes on society. The point at issue may perhaps be best understood by referring to figure 2. On the vertical axis for the diagram in panel A is depicted the total social benefits and total social costs of antitrust policy. On the horizontal axis is shown the degree of competition achieved by antitrust enforcement. The total costs

10. Later mathematical formulations of the theory of second best have shown that the decision rules for attaining optimality are so complex and the data necessary to implement these rules are so costly to obtain and so uncertain (if not totally unavailable) that Scherer branded the theory a "counsel of despair." F. M. Scherer, *Industrial Market Structure and Economic Performance* (Chicago: Rand McNally, 1970), p. 25.

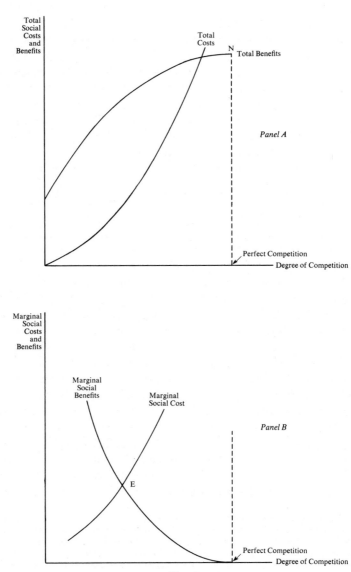

Figure 2

are those incurred by the federal antitrust enforcement agencies (the Antitrust Division of the Justice Department and the Federal Trade Commission), the costs of litigation and negotiation incurred by all plaintiffs and defendants, and the resources used in the administration of the courts. These costs include all resources expended by federal, state, and local governments and private parties involved in antitrust litigation and negotiation. They vary directly with antitrust enforcement. The greater the degree of enforcement, the greater the costs to society in the form of expended resources. What will be the shape of the curve showing the functional relation between the benefits of antitrust activity and the amount of enforcement? Similarly, what will be the shape of the curve showing the functional relationship between the amount of enforcement and the total costs of that enforcement?

The total benefit curve slopes upward and to the right because as more and more competition is brought about through antitrust activities, society's total welfare increases. The fact that the curve is concave from below indicates that society's benefits grow at a decreasing rate. Sensible antitrust policy would eliminate the worst inefficiencies first, in order to achieve the greatest welfare gains to society. Therefore, the benefits from optimal antitrust activity provide diminishing returns.[11] The total benefit curve reaches its peak at point N. Here perfect competition has been achieved; that is, prices equal marginal costs throughout the economy and total welfare is therefore maximized.

The total cost curve is upward sloping and convex from below. This configuration indicates that total costs rise with increasing antitrust enforcement as more and more of society's scarce resources are diverted to antitrust activities. The curve is convex from below because these

---

11. This conclusion is particularly realistic if the policy planners in the Antitrust Division and Federal Trade Commission rely more heavily than now is the case on concentration ratios as a starting point for information on questions of competition and monopoly. As the Census Bureau's concentration ratios increasingly become the hunting guide for detecting possible antitrust violations, the welfare losses from monopolistic behavior will tend to be reduced at a decreasing rate. A high official in the Justice Department has been quoted as asserting, "We are going to use [the Census data] quite a bit. Concentration data are tremendously important in our thinking process, picking which cases to bring and which to not." Cited in "Business Gets a New Measure of Bigness," *Business Week,* January 27, 1973, pp. 80–81.

costs grow at an increasing rate. The hypothesis that costs of antitrust activity grow at an increasing rate is consistent with the assertions of many legal scholars regarding the crisis in the federal court system resulting in part from antitrust litigation, especially increases in private cases.[12]

Panel B of figure 2 depicts the derivatives of the total cost and benefit functions of panel A. The optimal amount of antitrust enforcement from the point of view of society is determined at point E by the intersection of the marginal cost and marginal benefit curves. Note that this point of maximum net benefit falls short of the perfectly competitive solution. To attempt to push antitrust policy as far as perfect competition would mean that society gives up more in terms of resources than it receives from the benefits of greater competition. To move beyond the point of intersection of the marginal social benefit and cost curves, therefore, would involve an inefficient level of antitrust enforcement, as our theorem postulated.

Not since Philip Wicksteed told us how long to pray or how to allocate mashed potatoes at the dinner table have economists been so diligent in pushing their marginal tools into every nook and cranny of social behavior. Environmentalists are told how much sulphur dioxide must be allowed to remain in the air;[13] policemen are informed of the appropriate number of burglars who should remain at large;[14] consumers

12. Antitrust suits in United States courts of appeal have increased by 118 percent from 1968 to 1971 (compared to a 51 percent increase for all suits). See the *1971 Annual Report of the Director of the Administrative Office of the United States Courts* (1972), table 4. Antitrust civil cases in United States district courts have shown a large increase in the 1961–1971 decade: a 258 percent increase compared to 60 percent for all cases. See ibid., table 15. Suits by private plaintiffs make up the bulk of the increase in antitrust litigation; they have more than trebled in the past decade. See ibid., table 41. Antitrust cases are "big cases," that is, they use up a disproportionate quantity of judicial and litigative resources as evidenced by the high time study weight assigned them by the Administrative Office of the United States Courts. See ibid., table 33, also table C8.

13. Larry Ruff, "The Economic Common Sense of Pollution," *The Public Interest* (Spring 1970), p. 69; J. H. Dales, *Pollution, Property & Prices* (Toronto: University of Toronto Press, 1968).

14. See the remarks of Simon Rottenberg and Richard B. Hoffman in "Round Table on Allocation of Resources in Law Enforcement," *American Economic Review* (Proceedings) 59 (May 1969): 504; Thomas C. Schelling, "Economics and Criminal Enterprise," *The Public Interest* (Spring 1967), p. 61.

learn of the ideal number of pop bottles that may contain roaches or explode at will.[15] The hard-boiled economist feels efficient when he does not develop his golf game to Jack Nicklaus perfection and does not insist that all rivers and streams flow Vichy pure. Yet although he knows full well the fallacy in the old adage "if you can't do a thing well, don't do it at all," he still forgets the lesson of Wicksteed when discussing the efficient level of antitrust enforcement. For when it comes to the optimal degree of competition, except in the case of the theortical curiosa already noted, economists have been unable to see that there can be too much of even this good thing.

The Strategy of Antitrust Enforcement and Resource Utilization

The appropriate amount of resources devoted to antitrust activities is, as figure 2 has shown, determined by the intersection of the marginal social benefit and marginal social cost curves. If society is to the left of point E, then efficient economic policy would call for the expenditure of more resources in antitrust activity. On the other hand, if society is to the right of E, resources used in antitrust enforcement should be reduced in order to achieve the optimal degree of competition.

Precisely where the United States is in regard to point E is, of course, a most difficult matter to determine. Even those most conversant with the practices and policies of antitrust appear to differ. Many of them have implied that society is to the left of point E. For example, there have been numerous proposals to increase the scope of standing to include groups presently not eligible to sue for antitrust damages.[16] Enacting proposals of this sort would call forth much more litigation; presumably those urging their adoption are convinced that the result would be net gains to society. Other analyses of the standing to sue

15. James M. Buchanan, "In Defense of Caveat Emptor," *University of Chicago Law Review* 38 (Fall 1970): 64; Roland N. McKean, "Products Liability: Implications of Some Changing Property Rights," *Quarterly Journal of Economics* 84 (November 1970): 611.

16. See Bartlett H. McGuire, "The Passing-On Defense and the Right of Remote Purchasers to Recover Treble Damages Under Hanover Shoe," *University of Pittsburgh Law Review* 33 (Winter 1971): 177; and Comment, "Standing to Sue For Treble Damages Under Section 4 of The Clayton Act," *Columbia Law Review* 64 (March 1964): 570.

issue convey the impression that society is to the right of point E; they see very real dangers involved in the liberalization of the scope of standing.[17]

The legal literature contains the writings of many advocates of doctrines that would greatly expand the number of antitrust damage suits by both private parties and state governments.[18] One enthusiast has argued that "courts should allow all levels of consumer plaintiffs to establish at trial the fact of their damages."[19] But other experts are strongly opposed to such trends as expanded private class action suits in antitrust. In his 1971 annual antitrust review, Milton Handler concluded that there was then "little doubt that massive class actions constitute a net liability for antitrust, for federal courts, and for society generally."[20] Apparently joining him in placing society to the right of point E is a former acting head of the Antitrust Division who expressed misgivings about the likely impact of facilitating class actions and predicted a "proliferation of litigants" and "more congestion of the courts' dockets."[21] Three years later, F. M. Rowe, apparently believing that these predictions had come true, placed himself with those who believed society was to the right of point E by suggesting that expanded private antitrust

17. Earl E. Pollack, "The 'Injury' and 'Causation' Elements of a Treble Damage Antitrust Action," *Northwestern University Law Review* 57 (January-February 1963): 691; and "Automatic Treble Damages and the Passing-On Defense: The Hanover Shoe Decision," *Antitrust Bulletin* 13 (Winter 1968): 1183.

18. See, for example, Alan J. Howard, Comment, "Appealability of a Class Action Dismissal: The "Death Knell' Doctrine," *University of Chicago Law Review* 39 (Winter 1972): 403; Steward Shepherd, Comment, "Damage Distribution in Class Actions: The *Cy Pres* Remedy," *University of Chicago Law Review* 39 (Winter 1972): 448; Morris D. Forkosch, *Antitrust and the Consumer* (Buffalo: Dennis, 1956), pp. 311–344; and Comment, "Wrongs Without Remedy: The Concept of *Parens Patriae* Suits for Treble Damages Under the Antitrust Laws," *Southern California Law Review* 43 (1970): 570.

19. Comment, *"Mangano* and Ultimate Consumer Standing: The Misuse of the *Hanover* Doctrine," *Columbia Law Review* 72 (February 1972): 394, 414.

20. Milton Handler, "The Shift From Substantive to Procedural Innovation In Antitrust Suits—The Twenty-Third Annual Antitrust Review," *Columbia Law Review* 71 (January 1971): 1, 10. See also "Twenty-Fourth Annual Antitrust Review," *Columbia Law Review* 72 (January 1972): 1.

21. Walker B. Comegys, Jr., "The Advantages and Disadvantages of a Class Suit Under New Rule 23 As Seen by the Treble Damage Defendant," *Antitrust Law Journal* 32 (1966): 271, 277, 279.

efforts were "reminiscent of that dire prediction of Hobbes of the war by all against all."[22]

Although legal scholars disagree as to the precise location of the economy in terms of figure 2, economic theory does provide insight concerning the direction policy should take if society's goal is efficient allocation of scarce resources. Regardless of whether the economy is to the left or right of E, society should attempt to bring about any given degree of competition with instruments that require the least use of additional enforcement and litigation resources.

There is one very special condition under which the theorem itself would not hold. That condition arises when the degree of competition can be changed with no change in the amount of antitrust enforcement. If, for example, the budgets of the Antitrust Division and the Federal Trade Commission were held constant and the competitive impact of antitrust could still be increased, the theorem would be invalid. In such a case the marginal costs to society of this antitrust enforcement would be zero and therefore would be equated with the marginal benefits at perfect competition. Perfect competition then might be the appropriate social goal because it would coincide with the maximization of net benefits to society from antitrust enforcement. It follows, therefore, that the desire to efficiently use antitrust to bring about something approximating perfectly competitive conditions throughout the entire economy must eventually involve a policy that uses up the least amount of scarce resources. To what extent are the present weapons of antitrust enforcement consistent with this principle?

The present antitrust tool kit contains the following instruments for penalizing antitrust violations: (1) financial penalties paid to the state;[23] (2) treble damage payments to injured private parties;[24] (3) incarceration;[25] (4) the corporate surgery of dissolution, divorcement, and divestiture.[26] The efficacy of all these is affected by the amount of re-

---

22. F. M. Rowe, moderating ABA Antitrust Section 1969 annual meeting, as reported in *Antitrust Law Journal* 38 (1969): 720.
23. 15 U.S.C. §§ 1–2 (1970).
24. 15 U.S.C. § 15 (1970).
25. 15 U.S.C. §§ 1–2 (1970).
26. 15 U.S.C. § 4 (1970).

sources devoted to the detection and conviction of those guilty of anti-competitive behavior.[27]

Our purpose is to describe and analyze each of these measures in order to determine their probable deterrent effects and economic efficiency. Then it will be possible to suggest a program for modifying and streamlining the policy instruments in order to develop an antitrust approach that will maximize economic welfare and be consistent with the goal of approximating the benefits of perfect competition. A glance at the list of weapons indicates that they are an uneven assortment, the inevitable result of political accommodation emerging from the historical milieu of the period in which the Sherman Act was written. As the next chapter demonstrates, many of the penalties originally proposed did not survive the compromise package that the Sherman Act represents, and so our present arsenal does not by any means contain the whole range of possible weapons.

27. The reader will notice that there is no general category called injunctive relief in the list of antitrust instruments. Although injunctions other than structural relief often accompany court decisions in antitrust cases, such measures cannot be considered to be in the same category as the antitrust penalties. Injunctions to prevent and restrain antitrust violations can take many forms. For example, they might bar an antitrust violator from making future acquisitions, require that a certain percentage of his output be sold to small independent firms, or establish detailed credit arrangements for the sale of commodities covered by the court order. The possible injunctions are limitless, and each would have to be analyzed on its own merits. But since our analysis is not concerned with the benchmarks by which to appraise the anticompetitive or procompetitive implications of various antitrust decisions, we have self-consciously omitted injunctions other than structural relief. Structural relief, of course, does not involve the government in the detailed regulation of managerial decision making. Therefore it is a general instrument and has an appropriate place in the antitrust arena. Injunctive relief, on the other hand, is best treated under the rubric of government regulation.

2

THE REJECTED PENALTIES:
A HISTORICAL SURVEY

The records of the early congressional debates on antitrust, especially those concerning the Sherman Act, depict a Congress largely concerned with composing a law that would be both constitutional and favorably (or at least not adversely) affect the legislator and his party's political fortunes. The economic questions of the actual scope and impact of monopoly in the United States and the optimal means of deterring it or destroying its power were clearly ancillary issues.[1] Nevertheless, these and subsequent debates indicate that Congress has considered a sizable range of penalties. The debates also reveal much about the forces that caused Congress to decide on the final assortment. As mentioned earlier, a central purpose of this volume is to examine the economic implications of those penalties Congress ultimately levied. To that end chapters 3 and 4 are devoted specifically to the fine, the jail sentence, injunctive relief (notably dissolution, divorcement, and divestiture), and the private treble damage suit. Before appreciating where we are, however, it will be useful to know where we might have been. Only then can we proceed with confidence to where we want to be.

The Also Rans

Perhaps the most striking suggestion for penalizing the trusts (at one

1. The definitive treatise on the history of the antitrust deliberations is Hans B. Thorelli, *The Federal Antitrust Policy: Origination of an American Tradition* (Baltimore: Johns Hopkins Press, 1955). A scholarly, but somewhat more limited study is that of William Letwin, *Law and Economic Policy in America: The Evolution of the Sherman Act* (New York: Random House, 1965). See also Robert H. Bork, "Legislative Intent and the Policy of the Sherman Act," *Journal of Law & Economics* 9 (October, 1966): 7.

time profferred rather regularly) was to deny them the use of certain government facilities and institutions that were important (if not essential) in conducting business affairs. Favorable sentiment for such suggestions was most prominent after the *E. C. Knight* decision, which spurred some members of Congress to search for federal powers that could penalize trusts without running afoul of the Supreme Court's interstate commerce interpretations.[2] For example, Congressman Samuel Lanham of Texas observed that Congress's control over the mails could be employed to prevent the mailing of indecent or fraudulent material. Why, he asked rhetorically, could this same power not "be suitably directed against the contracts, the correspondence, the circulars, and all the epistolary and advertising agencies through which these illegal combinations . . . reach the individual or the public?"[3] Congressman George Ray of New York and his colleague Congressman William Terry of Arkansas introduced bills in the Fifty-sixth Congress that would have barred antitrust violators from the use of the postal system.[4] On May 31, 1900, a House joint resolution called for a constitutional amendment banning use of mails by the trusts.[5]

A similar and no less striking tack was taken by Senator George Gray of Delaware. His bill would have denied the trusts the use of the federal courts. Again, it was thought that Congress's ability to control the federal courts might enable this measure to pass constitutional muster.[6] The origins of this proposed penalty go back at least to Senator James George, a former Confederate general from Mississippi, who

2. *U.S. v. E. C. Knight,* 156 U.S. 1 (1895). In this decision, the American Sugar Refining Company, controlling 98 percent of the sugar refining production in the country, was absolved of Sherman Act charges brought by the government on the grounds that it was engaged in manufacturing, an activity distinct from commerce. Under this definition of commerce, only business firms that transported goods across state lines would be covered by the Sherman Act.

3. U.S., *Congressional Record,* 56th Cong., 1st. Sess., 1900, 331, part 7, 6325.

4. H. R. 9509, March 13, 1900; H. R. 11001, April 25, 1900. See U.S., Congress, Senate, *Bills and Debates in Congress Relating to Trusts,* 57th Cong., 2d Sess., 1903, pp. 625 and 885 respectively (hereafter cited as B & D). See also Congressman John W. Gaines's defense of the constitutionality of this measure. U.S., *Congressional Record,* 56th Cong., 1st Sess., 1900, xxxiii, appendix, 276–279.

5. U.S., *Congressional Record,* 56th Cong., 1st Sess., 1900, 33, part 7, 6304–6305.

6. Thorelli, *Federal Antitrust Policy,* p. 196.

once stated his intention to introduce an amendment (to Senator John Sherman's original bill) that would prevent trusts from gaining any access to the courts of the United States.[7]

Running parallel to denying antitrust violators the use of the mail or the courts are the early congressional proposals denying them the right to ship or transport their wares. There were suggestions simply to prohibit the interstate shipments of trust-made goods.[8] The specific mechanism for barring these shipments was not always made clear, though their seizure by a United States marshal was proposed. Congressman Thomas Ball of Texas, no doubt questioning whether Congress had the power to simply shut off the interstate shipment of goods and services, proposed that the penalty be placed instead upon those firms shipping the products of antitrust violators. He argued that since Congress had the power to regulate interstate commerce, it was logical to penalize the trusts through a punishment one step removed. If firms that knowingly transported goods controlled by monopolies were fined, Ball believed, shippers would refuse to carry these goods, thus ending monopoly power. Senator Shelby Cullom of Illinois, the first legislator to use the term "antitrust," introduced a bill that attacked the transportation problem at both ends. A firm violating the antitrust laws was to be prohibited from transporting its merchandise outside its home state and forever enjoined from engaging in interstate commerce. Any carriers caught transporting a violator's wares would also be eligible for substantial fines.[9] The decision in the *E. C. Knight* case was an obvious impetus for this penalty.

A number of suggestions were made proposing forfeiture to the government of the merchandise of firms that violated the antitrust laws. Indiana Senator David Turpie provided the most straightforward proposal:

> Resolved, that the proposed penal enactments against trusts . . . should provide for the seizure of trust goods . . . and for the for-

---

7. Ibid., p. 173. Senator George, a devoted states' righter, may have thought so outrageous a penalty would scuttle the antitrust legislation. He was Senator Sherman's most dogged critic, questioning the constitutionality as well as the desirability of the proposed legislation against the trusts.
8. Thorelli, *Federal Antitrust Policy*, p. 513.
9. S. 6323, Dec. 2, 1902, as reported in ibid., p. 531.

feiture, confiscation, and the sale of the same upon due process of trial and hearing . . .[10]

Turpie introduced this resolution during the debates on the original Sherman bill; and, although he indicated his general sympathy for anti-monopoly legislation, he stressed his desire that a forfeiture penalty be appended to any antitrust law. Provisions in the trust legislation proposed by Congressman Ray and Terry also contained forfeiture provisions.[11]

A forfeiture penalty did make its way into the Sherman Act. Section 6 of that statute still provides that

> Any property owned under any contract or by any combination, or pursuant to any conspiracy . . . mentioned in section one of this act, and being in the course of transportation from one State to another, or to a foreign country, shall be forfeited to the United States, and may be seized and condemned . . .

Taken literally, this section would adversely affect a trust only if its merchandise could be seized in transit. Senator George had argued that this language assured the penalty's ineffectiveness. Later proposals for forfeiture tried to expand the penalty's scope, but they were unsuccessful. Section 6 is thus a dead letter; it has been used no more than three or four times since the act's inception.[12]

Antitrust forfeiture does make an appearance in other legislation. For example, Public Law 151, a statute concerned with encouraging the development of coal deposits, contains a provision for the forfeiture of coal deposit lands acquired in Alaska if any of the lands or deposits are controlled by unlawful trusts or are part of a conspiracy in restraint of trade in the mining or selling of coal.[13]

Forfeiture was one of the original penalties levied against monopolistic activity. The first recorded antimonopoly law is the edict of the Roman Emperor Zeno, issued about fourteen hundred years prior to the Sher-

10. Ibid., p. 175.
11. Ibid., see also the bill by F. H. Gillett: H.R. 10249, February 5, 1897, B & D, p. 551.
12. Walton Hamilton, U.S., Congress, House Committee on the Judiciary, *Hearings, Study of Monopoly Power,* 81st Cong., 1st Sess., part 1, 1949, p. 287.
13. 35 Stat. 424.

man Act; and the first penalty mentioned for imposition on those who "shall presume to practice a monopoly" is the forfeiture of property.[14] The second penalty in Zeno's edict is even starker: The violator is to be condemned to perpetual exile.[15]

As it was in Zeno's time, the forfeiture penalty is a harsh, blunt instrument, and it may have been perversely proposed for that very reason. Walton Hamilton argued that Senator John Morgan of Alabama secretly hoped that the seizure and confiscation penalties that he recommended would encourage the Supreme Court to hold the antitrust laws unconstitutional.[16]

The hypothesis that the tariff is the "mother of the trusts" was commonly mentioned during the early deliberations on the monopoly problem. It is thus not surprising that some legislators urged that tariff reduction or elimination be incorporated as a penalty against the trusts. Thorelli counted eight bills introduced in 1890 in the House of Representatives alone that were "based in whole or in part on the idea of tariff reductions or suspension with regard to trust-controlled or similar goods."[17] Proposals for the enactment of this device usually came from members of the Democratic party. Early representatives of these are the bills of Kentucky's William Breckinridge and North Carolina's John Henderson.[18] Senator Sherman, the central figure in the trust legislation on the Senate side, also expressed early support for this penalty. The most comprehensive support, however, came from Senator George Vest, a Democrat from Missouri. Vest was persuaded that tariff reduction was the only constitutional remedy that could be applied against the

14. See testimony of Frank A. Fetter, *Hearings, Investigation of Concentration of Economic Power,* Temp. Nat. Econ. Comm., 76th Cong., 1st Sess., part 5, 1939, pp. 1658–1659.
15. Even this stricture is not without a Sherman Act counterpart. Public Law 197 (41 Stat. 594), passed by the 66th Congress, provided for deportation of any alien convicted of a Sherman Act charge in aid of a belligerent in the European War. It was in force from August 1, 1914, to April 6, 1917.
16. Hamilton, *Hearings, Study of Monopoly Power,* p. 287.
17. Thorelli, *Federal Antitrust Policy,* pp. 175–176.
18. See H. R. 8036, March 5, 1888, and H. R. 11395, September 10, 1888 in *B & D,* pp. 45–46 and 63 respectively. For one of the rare Republican proposals, see Maryland Congressman George Pearre's bill: H.R. 6072, January 12, 1900, *B & D,* p. 615.

trusts. He also felt the remedy would be effective and supported his belief by listing twenty different trusts that were protected by high tariffs.[19] A typical mechanism for implementing this particular instrument is found in a House joint resolution of 1900 for an antitrust amendment to the Constitution. Section 12 would have allowed the president to suspend duties or import taxes on products whose prices had been enhanced by monopoly.[20]

Senator Sherman had originally argued that taxation provided the only constitutional basis available to the Congress for thwarting the trusts. While Sherman later abandoned his advocacy of this penalty, others continued to suggest the levying of taxes upon either the trusts or their output as a viable antitrust instrument.[21] And this sentiment did not cease with the passage of the Sherman Act. Senator R. F. Pettigrew, a Republican from South Dakota, in complaining that some trusts (such as Standard Oil) were not affected by tariffs, argued that

> a tax upon their gross product could be levied by Congress, and thereby those trusts would be compelled to dissolve, because the burden of taxation would give to the individual sufficient advantage so that he could compete with the great trusts [and] thus drive them out of business.[22]

Without doubt, the most bizarre tax proposal was made by the Kansas Democrat and Populist Edwin Ridgely. His bill would have levied a progressive tax on the total value of the stocks and bonds of a corporation but would have permitted corporations to merge in order to increase "their ability to command a better price for their products . . ."[23]

To a contemporary observer, one of the most interesting aspects of the government's deliberations about thwarting the trusts is the emphasis upon the "weapon" of publicity. In keeping with Brandeis's well known quip that sunlight is the best of disinfectants, a number of public servants seemed to believe that enough publicity, even in the form of straight-

19. See Thorelli, *Federal Antitrust Policy,* p. 187.
20. Ibid., citing 33 Cong. Rec. 6304–6305.
21. Ibid., pp. 173–174, esp. n. 29.
22. 33 Cong. Rec. 6582, as quoted in ibid., p. 526.
23. H.R. 5756, January 10, 1900; *B & D,* p. 613.

orward documentation about the monopoly problem, would constitute n effective antitrust weapon. The value of this instrument was especially •opular in the early 1900s and was regularly espoused by Theodore Roosevelt. The publicity measures generally were to operate through a mechanism of federal licensing of corporations, through federal inspection of corporate records, or both. Roosevelt, taking his cue from the overnment examination of banks, said that, after the inspection of great orporations,

> wherever the interests of the public demand it, [the State] should publish the results of its examination. Then, if there are inordinate profits, competition or public sentiment will give the public the benefit of lowered prices; and if not the power of taxation remains. It is therefore evident that publicity is the one sure and adequate remedy which we can now invoke. There may be other remedies, but what these others are we can only find out by publicity, as the result of investigation. The first requisite is knowledge, full and complete.[24]

The Bureau of Corporations, established in 1903 as a part of the Department of Commerce and Labor, was President Roosevelt's vehicle or producing the "daylight" that he considered the basis of a viable ntitrust program. According to Letwin, the bureau was to inform the president of its corporate investigations, and Roosevelt would then publicize those business activities he considered pernicious.[25] Letwin's nterpretation here is probably correct, for Theodore Roosevelt was nown to be persuaded of the clear distinction between the good and he bad trust.

The most extreme example of the publicity approach is found in a ill submitted by Congressman David De Armond of Missouri. His nusual proposal would have required marking upon every product hipped in interstate commerce the statement that the product was not a nonopoly product and had been produced in open competition.[26] A

24. As quoted in Thorelli, *Federal Antitrust Policy*, p. 415.
25. Letwin, *Law and Economic Policy*, pp. 240–241.
26. H.R. 15923, December 11, 1902, as reported in Thorelli, *Federal Antitrust olicy*, p. 533.

milder approach was suggested by Senator George Shoup of Idaho.
Shoup introduced legislation that would have penalized every businessman who did not keep a copy of the Sherman Act prominently posted
at his place of business.[27]

Economists played an insignificant role in the early trust legislation.
No economist testified in behalf of the antimonopoly bills that were introduced in the latter part of the nineteenth century. Furthermore,
judging from the professional literature, few economists seemed aware
of or concerned with the welfare implications of the concentration and
merger movement. Thus it is interesting to note, as Thorelli documents,
that when economists first began to write about the trust, the instrument
they generally recommended for its deterrence was publicity.[28] For
example, Henry Carter Adams, one of the most influential American
economists of the time, concluded that

> from whatever point of view the trust problem is considered,
> publicity stands as the first step in its solution; and there is reason
> to believe that the further the government is willing to go in its
> statutory definition of publicity the greater likelihood is there that
> it may be excused from the necessity of exercising direct admin-
> istrative control.[29]

Similarly, Arthur T. Hadley, another prominent American economist
and former president of Yale University, while noting the ineffectiveness
of statutory approaches to ending monopoly, asserted the value of
publicity.[30]

American economists gave their first definitive sign of recognition of
the trust problem at their twelfth annual convention in 1899. The
dominant topic of this meeting, held in Ithaca, was the trust problem.
Publicity—which Thorelli humorously suggests is a rather self-serving

27. S. 1346, March 29, 1897; *B & D*, p. 555.
28. Thorelli, *Federal Antitrust Policy*, pp. 320–323.
29. Henry C. Adams, "What is Publicity," *North American Review* 175 (De
cember 1902): 895–904; at 904 cited in Thorelli, *Federal Antitrust Policy*
pp. 321.
30. Arthur T. Hadley, "The Good and Evil of Industrial Combination," *At
lantic Monthly* 79 (March 1897): 377–385, cited in Thorelli, *Federal Antitrus
Policy*, pp. 322–323.

policy for economists to recommend—was the primary policy espoused to cope with the trusts.[31]

Certainly the most unusual device for gaining publicity and information about the trusts was Congressman Jack Beall's bill to give rewards to informers who exposed antitrust violations.[32] The idea was not original with the Texas congressman, however, but had been created by Henry B. Martin, the national secretary of the Antitrust League. This bill would have given 10 percent of all fines, forfeitures, and penalties to the informant. Henry Martin pointed to the $100,000 reward paid to a Mr. Parr for information about violations of customs laws by the sugar trust—which led to a $2 million recovery by the Treasury—and concluded that such rewards are "well established in the legislation of all civilized countries of the world."[33] Other proposals, if enacted, would have compelled the involuntary bankruptcy of every corporation attempting to monopolize and the levy of a 10 percent capitalization tax on any company that could not show it was complying with the Sherman Act.

It seems probable that, however inadvertent it might have been, Congress showed good judgment in rejecting the use of most of the unusual penalties just adumbrated. To bar trusts from the use of such facilities as the federal courts and the mails is an unusually blunt instrument. Though their creators were motivated by a desire to construct a penalty impervious to Court attack, these measures would likely have violated the due process provision of the Constitution. And from an economic standpoint the instruments are not efficient: they would require the cessation of the business altogether, probably costing the consumer more in consumer's surplus than the welfare lost as a result of the monopoly. Moreover, the bills, if enacted, probably would have met the same fate as the only denial penalty on the books, the Panama Canal Act. That act, passed by the Sixty-second Congress, provides that

31. See Papers and Proceedings, *Publications of the American Economic Association,* vol. 1 (3d Series, 1899).
32. H.R. 20194, April 1, 1912. See U.S., Congress, House, Committee on the Judiciary, *Hearings, Rewards for Information of Violation of Antitrust Law,* 62nd Cong., 2d Sess., 1912.
33. Ibid., Testimony of Mr. Henry B. Martin, p. 7.

ships owned by companies doing business in violation of the antitrust laws may not use the Panama Canal. Congress had apparently hoped that the 9,000-mile detour around the Horn would prove so costly to monopolists that they would forego their anticompetitive ways.[34] The provision has hardly become the mainstay of vigorous antitrust enforcement.

As an appropriate deterrent to anticompetitive activity, banning the shipment of monopoly-produced merchandise has little to commend itself from a cost standpoint. A mechanism adequate to police and intercept interstate shipments would have to be added to the social mechanism that ferrets out the antitrust violation itself.

That forfeiture was supported by some opponents of antitrust and that this Sherman Act stricture has been virtually unused attests to its impotence. Forfeiture, like the interception of shipments, involves the government in the identification, confiscation, gathering, and sale of merchandise. Solving issues of which goods are eligible for forfeiture would be relatively costly compared to the implementation of other penalties. There is no conceptual difference from the firm's standpoint between requiring it to forfeit a certain percentage of its assets or inventory and requiring it to pay a certain fine. As we shall later demonstrate, there is, however, an important difference from society's standpoint. The same is true of another penalty never adopted, namely placing a tax on monopolists—which is tantamount to fining them.

Removing tariffs makes economic sense irrespective of the degree of concentration, and it is unfortunate that such measures were not adopted. However, as a device to specifically penalize monopoly power, tariff reduction is unwieldy. Even if adopted, it would not affect monopolists in markets not subject to foreign competition. Moreover, it is an indiscriminate instrument that would penalize the innocent along with the guilty.

Antitrust observers today seem rather unenthusiastic about reliance on the instrument of publicity. The belief that publicity can remedy an onerous situation remains a part of American folklore—but today such beliefs mainly relate to political phenomena. Witness the credit given to

34. 37 Stat. 567; 49 U.S.C. 5 (14).

the press for its alleged uncovering of the Watergate affair.[35] However, economic problems are more intractable. They are not likely simply to go away because publicity has been focused upon them.

To be fair, some of the pleas for publicity about the trusts were simply requests for information that could be used in dispassionately analyzing these corporations so that effective remedies could be taken against any malefactors. But among many observers, including professional economists, there was then the naive belief that a person would do good, if only he were informed about what the good was. The view that the managements of large corporations could be relied upon to behave in the public interest, and that mere publicity about their actions would foster social responsibility, today seems a quaint doctrine whose adherents are concentrated largely in the nation's business schools.[36]

The Congressional Concern

The early debates leading to the passage of the Sherman Act showed only a tangential concern with the actual means of deterring monopoly. While this focus turned out to be regrettable, it is not surprising. There were legislators who were not enthusiastic about enacting any viable antitrust legislation. Senator Orville Platt correctly charged that some occupants of the Capitol were mindful only of passing some bill that could be "headed 'A bill to punish trusts' with which to go to the country."[37] But others, genuinely concerned about the trust problem, tended to overlook the penalties issue because of ignorance, an ignor-

35. For a rebuttal to the view that publicity, especially that generated by the news media, actually exposes political chicanery, see two perceptive articles by Edward Jay Epstein, "Did the Press Uncover Watergate?" *Commentary* 58 (July 1974): 21–24; and "Journalism and Truth" *Commentary* 57 (April 1974): 36–40.

36. To be sure, corporate managers can find publicity unpleasant. Ralph Cordiner, the board chairman of General Electric at the time of the electrical equipment conspiracies, no doubt found it more than inconvenient when the University of Massachusetts rejected him as a candidate for an honorary degree because of General Electric's antitrust difficulties. See UPI Report of February 16, 1961, as cited in Comment, "Increasing Community Control over Corporate Crime—A Problem in The Law of Sanctions," *Yale Law Journal* 71 (January 1961): 280.

37. Thorelli, *Federal Antitrust Policy*, p. 198.

ance attributable not to shirking but to inexperience with the problem. Compounding the ignorance and inexperience in the legislative branch at the time was the virtual absence of any analysis by economists of efficient methods of deterring monopoly.

Also occupying the congressional center stage, and resulting in flourishes of delightful oratory was the battle between the Republicans and Democrats over who would gain the credit for antitrust legislation. Congressman William Terry chided the Republicans:

> Even now the trust magnates who fill your campaign coffers are laughing at the high antics you are cutting up. You frame constitutional amendments and put anti-trust planks in your platforms, but the trusts are not scared even a little bit at any such performances. They know that all your noise is only stage thunder; that it is "only thunder in the index," and that the after chapters will be entirely lovely and serene.[38]

He and other Democrats spent much of their time in speechmaking trying to assure that the "party of the trusts" would not receive acclaim as the party of the people as well. Senator Sherman, after all, was a Republican. In such an atmosphere, those legislators who did find time to give serious consideration to the drafting of a sound antitrust bill tended to be unusually occupied (not without merit, it turned out) with the constitutional issue of Congress's power to legislate against the trusts; they were not mindful of the penalties issue.

Later deliberations on the trust question, especially those after the *E. C. Knight* decision and the Supreme Court's rendition of the rule of reason in the *Standard Oil* and *American Tobacco* cases, brought the weaknesses of the Sherman Act under intense scrutiny. Unfortunately, the level of the debate on deterrence did not then reach a higher plane. By this time, especially during the Roosevelt era, the remedy for the perceived failure of the Sherman Act was not seen in more stringent penalties but rather in government regulation of a more direct and pervasive nature. This sort of regulation was one of the key elements in

---

38. U.S. *Congressional Record,* 56th Cong., 1st Sess., 1900, 33, Part 7, 6319. Aside from mixing metaphors, the Congressman seems clearly to have confused a book's Index with its Table of Contents.

Roosevelt's economic policy after his disenchantment with the judicial approach to curbing monopoly. President Roosevelt's messages to Congress in 1907 and 1908 stressed the need for an administrative agency modeled after the recently established Interstate Commerce Commission or Comptroller of the Currency, which would make its "prohibitions and permissions as clear and definite as possible." The historic 1907 Chicago Conference on Trusts, which was attended by economists, businessmen, and labor leaders, also stressed the regulation rather than the deterrence of monopolistic practices.[39] The upshot of this conference was the Hepburn bill, which neglected the question of viable penalties and concentrated on the means of overseeing and approving business agreements and transactions by government commission.[40] Although 1914 saw passage of the Federal Trade Commission Act, which established an administrative agency, and the Clayton Act, which barred specified anticompetitive practices, neither, of course, stressed the penalties side of antitrust enforcement.

Since the passage of those two acts, the level of interest in the monopoly problem generally has subsided. And the proposals for deterring and remedying the problem of monopoly never displayed the variety and rambunctiousness of those of the earlier era. This is not to say that interest in improving the instruments of antitrust ebbed away. Rather the debates, academic and political, economic and legal, have since been constrained to modifying those penalties which evolved in and survived the 1890—1914 legislative period: fines, jails, structural relief (the public actions), and treble damages (the private approach).

---

39. Proceedings of the National Conference on Trusts and Combinations. Held under the auspices of the National Civic Federation, Chicago, October 22–25, 1907 (1908), as reported in Arthur M. Johnson, "Antitrust Policy in Transition, 1908: Ideal and Reality" *Mississippi Valley Historical Review* 48 (December 1961): 415.

40. H.R. 19745, 60th Cong., 1st Sess., as reported in Letwin, *Law and Economic Policy*, p. 248.

3

THE PUBLIC ACTION PENALTIES: INCARCERATION, STRUCTURAL RELIEF, FINES

The Incarceration Penalty

"Go directly to jail, do not pass Go, do not collect $200." These celebrated words from a chance card used in Parker Brothers' game of Monopoly probably have led generations of youngsters to grow up believing that "monopoly" and "going directly to jail" are inevitably linked. But when John Marvin Cook, vice president in charge of marketing for the Cutler-Hammer Corporation, was sentenced to a thirty-day jail term by Federal District Judge J. Cullen Ganey in the largest antitrust criminal action in history (the electrical equipment conspiracy), Cook did not "go directly to jail." His circuitous route involved a seven-day delay and a stop-off to attend his daughter's engagement party, the real life equivalent, perhaps, of passing Go and collecting $200.[1]

Judge Ganey's leniency to the defendant in this matter is indicative of the relaxed attitude that prevails toward imprisonment as a punishment for antitrust violators. This nonchalance has existed since the prison penalty was inserted in the Sherman Act. Although for eighty-five years the act provided the possibility of imprisonment for a period up to one year on each count of the indictment, incarceration for an antitrust

---

1. John G. Fuller, *The Gentlemen Conspirators* (New York: Grove Press, 1962), p. 100. Cook's sentence (as well as those of all others involved in the electrical equipment cases) was later reduced to twenty-five days. See *Industrial Control Equipment Case* (Bluebook number 1539) for a summary of the issues and sentences meted out in the case involving Cook.

offense has not been common.[2] Thus, from 1890 to 1940—the first fifty years of Sherman Act enforcement—there were 24 cases involving jail sentences out of 252 criminal prosecutions. Only 11 of these cases involved businessmen (the others being trade union leaders). More significantly, 10 of these 11 cases involved acts of violence, threats, or other forms of intimidation, and the remaining jail sentence was suspended.[3]

During the next fifteen years (1940 to 1955) prison sentences were imposed in eleven Sherman Act criminal cases, but in almost every case the sentences were suspended.[4] The period 1955 to 1959 is important in the history of criminal penalties imposed under the Sherman Act because at the end of that interval the first prison sentence for price fixing alone (i.e., involving no acts of violence or union misconduct) occurred.[5] The landmark 1959 case involved five corporations that were charged with conspiring to fix the price of hand tools and eliminate competition in the sale of these instruments. The defendants allegedly had adopted uniform noncompetitive prices, basing points, shipping terms, and freight charges; they had also standardized specifications. These offenses did not differ in economic significance from the types of

2. Section 14 of the Clayton Act also provides for the possibility of imprisonment for antitrust violations: "Whenever a corporation shall violate any of the penal provisions of the antitrust laws, such violation shall be deemed to be also that of the individual directors, officers, or agents of such corporation who shall have authorized, ordered, or done any of the acts constituting in whole or in part such violation and such violations shall be deemed a misdemeanor, and upon conviction therefore of any such director, officer, or agent, he shall be punished by a fine of not exceeding $5,000 or by imprisonment for not exceeding one year, or by both, in the discretion of the court" (15 U.S.C. 24 [1958]). Notwithstanding this provision, the government has always chosen to indict corporate officials under section 1, 2, or 3 of the Sherman Act. Section 14 of the Clayton Act has yet to be used to bring corporate officials to trial. Richard A. Whiting, "Antitrust and the Corporate Executive," *Virginia Law Review* 47 (October 1961): 929, 942.

3. U.S., Congress, House, Committee on Small Business, Monopoly Subcommittee, *United States Versus Economic Concentration and Monopoly,* 79th Cong., 2d Sess., 1946, p. 257.

4. CCH, *The Federal Antitrust Laws With Summary of Cases Instituted by the United States, 1890–1951* (1952); 1952–1956 supp. (1957).

5. See James M. Clabault and John F. Burton, Jr., *Sherman Act Indictments 1955–1965: A Legal and Economic Analysis* (New York: Federal Legal Publications, 1966), pp. 40–41.

activities involved in cases that preceded it. Indeed the government (believing perhaps that by this time the prison penalty for Sherman Act infringements was a dead letter) did not even recommend prison terms for the individuals involved. Nevertheless (and in spite of pleas of *nolo contendere* on the part of the defendants), the court imposed a ninety-day prison term on four individuals and fined each $5,000. Shocked by the unprecedented severity of the sentence, the defendants attempted to change their plea to not guilty and stand trial, but their motions were rejected.[6]

The next year, 1960, witnessed the most dramatic episode in the history of the Sherman Act, the advent of the electrical equipment cases, which involved every major corporation in that industry. Briefly, these cases included forty-five individual and twenty-nine corporate defendants and comprised twenty separate indictments. In all, seven company officials were given thirty-day jail terms.[7] In 1966, near the termination of these cases, Clabault and Burton expressed their belief that from that time on "antitrust would never be quite the same again."[8] Others shared the view that jail sentences in *McDonough* and the electrical equipment cases heralded a new era.[9]

But this prediction proved false. In the period since the imposition of the prison terms in the electrical equipment cases, few sentences have resulted in imprisonment. Most have been suspended or served on probation. During these eight years (1966 to 1974), only eighteen cases have resulted in the imposition of jail sentences or probation. In only

6. One of the defendants, John T. Main, en route to surrender himself to the custody of the United States marshal who would deliver him to the federal penitentiary at Milan, Michigan, stopped his car, excused himself from the presence of his family on the pretense of regaining his composure, and fatally shot himself. Of this event, Ralph Nader's study group on antitrust enforcement commented, "the well-publicized incident cooled any inclination judges did retain toward prison sentences." Mark J. Green, et al., *The Closed Enterprise System* (New York: Grossman Publishers, 1972), p. 168n.

7. Clabault and Burton, *Sherman Act Indictments,* p. 45. This book provides a summary of the cases involved in the electrical equipment conspiracy as well as all cases involving the penal sanction for antitrust violations from 1955 to 1965.

8. Ibid.

9. Harry V. Ball and Lawrence M. Friedman, "The Use of Criminal Sanctions in the Enforcement of Economic Legislation: A Sociological View," *Stanford Law Review* 17 (January 1965): 197.

seven of these were jail terms actually served.[10] Table 1 summarizes the recent cases involving penal sanctions. It convincingly demonstrates that the enthusiasm of judges to impose prison sentences has been no greater than it was before the electrical equipment cases.

This table of recent cases, as well as the evidence available since 1890, clearly reveals that judges are reluctant to impose prison sentences for antitrust violations, even though imprisonment is one of the oldest and least debated of all the antitrust penalties. Incarceration was not only provided for in the final version of the Sherman Act, as drafted by the Judiciary Committee, but was also a part of Senator Sherman's original proposal.[11]

There was in fact no debate at all on the question of whether there should be prison terms for violations of the antitrust laws. Indeed, most of the bills introduced to deal with monopolistic practices provided for even tougher imprisonment measures than did the version of the bill that finally passed. Senator John Reagan's alternative bill, offered on August 14, 1888, proposed that any persons associated with a trust should "be guilty of a high misdemeanor" and be liable for fines and imprisonment of "not more than five years and not less than one year."[12] Horace Chilton, Reagan's successor in the Senate, wanted to punish for not more than three years every person knowingly involved in the transportation of articles that were produced by combinations in restraint of trade.[13] Congressman William Greene of Nebraska offered a slightly revised version of the Sherman Act, amending section 1 to make restraints of trade by combination a felony punishable by imprisonment for not less than two years nor more than fifteen. The penalty in section 2 would have been similarly increased.[14] But even Greene's strong feelings on the matter were no match for those of Congressman John Little of Arkansas. Little wanted any persons participating in the formation

---

10. In the decade 1955 to 1965, twenty-six cases resulted in jail sentences or probation; in only six were jail sentences actually served. See Clabault and Burton, *Sherman Act Indictments,* esp. p. 55.

11. William Letwin, *Law and Economic Policy in America: The Evolution of the Sherman Antitrust Act* (New York: Random House, 1965), p. 90.

12. Hans B. Thorelli, *The Federal Antitrust Policy: Origination of an American Tradition* (Baltimore: Johns Hopkins Press, 1955), pp. 169–170.

13. Ibid., p. 509.

14. Ibid., p. 510.

Table 1. Recent Antitrust Cases Involving Penal Sanctions

Blue Book Number	Case	Year Case Instituted	Product Line	Names of Individual Defendants	Jail Sentence Imposed	Time to Be Served	Probation Time
1884	*United States v. D.D. Bean & Sons Co., et al.*	1966	Book matches	Irvin H. Koenig	90 days	None	1 day
				Richard J. Walters	30 days	None	1 day
				Harold Meiters	30 days	None	1 day
				D. D. Bean, Jr.	90 days	None	1 day
1990	*United States v. American Radiator & Standard Corp., et al.*	1966	Plumbing fixtures	Robert E. Casner	1 year	15 days	2 years
				Stanley S. Backner	6 months	24 hours	1 year
				Robert J. Pierson, Jr.	3 months	None	1 year
				John B. Balmer	1 year	30 days	2 years
				George W. Kelch	9 months	7 days	2 years
				Joseph J. Decker	1 year	60 days	3 years
				Daniel J. Quinn	1 year	1 day	1 year
				Norman R. Held	1 year	50 days	1 year
1954	*United States v. Globe Ticket Co., et al.*	1967	Theater and athletic event tickets	Frank W. Rugg	1 year	None	1 year
				H. Stanley Heeb	suspended	None	1 year
				William F. Gillenwater	suspended	None	6 months
				Wilber Startzman	suspended	None	1 year
				Vincent D. Brislane	suspended	None	6 months
				James S. Arcus, Jr.	suspended	None	1 year
				John B. Elliott	suspended	None	6 months
				Clifford Elliott	6 months	None	6 months
				Milton Manshel	6 months	None	1 year
				Thomas Leonard	suspended	None	6 months
				E. W. Taylor	1 year	None	1 year
1963A	*United States v. American Bakeries Co., et al.*	1967	Bread and baked goods	Norman V. Clexton	7 months	None	1 year
				Ray W. Moore	7 months	None	1 year

No.	Case	Year	Product	Defendant			
1997	United States v. General Host Corp., et al.	1968	Bread	Charles A. Stewart	7 months	None	1 year
				Samuel A. McLaughlin	7 months	None	1 year
				William J. Coughlin	5 months	None	10 months
				Harold C. Overholt	5 months	None	10 months
				L. S. Parsons	5 months	None	10 months
				Russell E. Kisor	5 months	None	10 months
				Donald O. Roskam	5 months	None	10 months
				John H. Way, Sr.	8 months	None	1 year
				Robert Bohringer	None	None	1 month
				Eugene J. Gase, Jr.	None	None	6 months
2032	United States v. Circle Floor, Inc., et al.	1968	Installation of maple floors in gyms and auditoriums	Earl E. Campbell	1 year	None	1 year
				James T. Scott	1 year	None	1 year
				Oscar Clouser	1 year	None	1 year
				Leo M. Roussel	1 year	None	1 year
				Harry B. Konn	1 year	None	1 year
				W. R. Schilling	1 year	None	1 year
				Julius Heim	1 month	None	1 year
				George Huber, Jr.	2 months	None	1 year
				Otto Berk, Jr.	1 year	None	2 years
2054	United States v. Dunham Concrete Products, Inc., et al.	1969	Concrete products	Ted F. Dunham, Jr.	6 months	6 months	None
2090	United States v. Charles W. Bengimina, et al.	1970	Vending machine products	Charles W. Bengimina	1 year	3 months	3 years
				Nicholas Evola	1 year	1 month	3 years
2124	United States v. Metro Denver Concrete Assn., et al.	1970	Ready-mix concrete	Melvin W. Flanagan	7 months	1 month	1 year
				Arthur J. Clark	7 months	1 month	1 year
				Frank P. Spratlen III	7 months	1 month	1 year

Table 1 (*Continued*)

Blue Book Number	Case	Year Case Instituted	Product Line	Names of Individual Defendants	Jail Sentence Imposed	Time to Be Served	Probation Time
2136	*United States v. Richter Concrete Corp., et al.*	1970	Ready-mix concrete	Thomas W. Meade	7 months	1 month	1 year
				Charles R. Eatchel	7 months	1 month	1 year
2145	*United States v. Darling-Delaware, Inc., et al.*	1970	Rendering raw materials into tallow, grease, feed, fertilizer	Eddie K. Wilson	None	None	2 years
				Irwin Frisch	suspended	None	6 months
				Charles L. Hausserman, Jr.	6 months	None	1 year
				Herman Isacs III	3 months	None	1 year
				John Lee Isacs	suspended	None	6 months
				Robert E. Kohn	30 days	None	6 months
				Albert Mosthof	suspended	None	6 months
				William J. Rosenberg	3 months	None	1 year
				Melvin M. Sachs	3 months	None	6 months
				George J. Schaming	6 months	None	1 year
				H. Clay Stahler	3 months	None	1 year
				Harry Theobald	6 months	None	1 year
				Irving Block	6 months	None	1 year
2163	*United States v. National Association for Air Freighting, Inc., et al.*	1971	Import air freight	Jack F. Sarcona	None	None	2 years
				Haskell Wolf	None	None	2 years
				Frank Yandolino	None	None	2 years
2213	*United States v. Garage Door Manufacturers Assn., Inc., et al.*	1972	Overhead garage doors	George P. Cain	30 days	None	None
				Irv Snyder	30 days	None	None

2243	United States v. Clark Mechanical Contractors, Inc., et al.	1972	Mechanical contracting supplies for installing plumbing, pipe fitting, sheet metal work	Richard F. Clark	30 days	30 days	None
				William R. Ward	9 months	9 months	None
				James E. Smith, Jr.	30 days	30 days	None
				Paul Jeanes, Jr.	30 days	30 days	None
				Coleman Waltrip	30 days	30 days	None
				Charles M. Koenig	30 days	30 days	None
2278	United States v. Blue Ribbon Meat Co., et al.	1972	Wholesale meat	Leonard H. Harris	30 days	30 days	None
2280	United States v. Gonnella Baking Co., et al.	1972	Bread baking (Italian, French, and Vienna style)	Louis L. Marcucci	None	None	1 year
				George D. Marcucci	None	None	1 year
				Lawrence L. Marcucci	None	None	1 year
2305	United States v. Jahncke Service, Inc., et al.	1973	Ready-mix concrete	Herbert G. Jahncke, Sr.	30 days	30 days	1 year
				Frank T. Dooley	30 days	30 days	1 year
				Edward N. Lennox	30 days	30 days	1 year
2339	United States v. Austin Steel Co., Inc., et al.	1973	Reinforcing steel bars	Roger Montgomery	1 year	None	18 months
				Allen Huff Hines	1 year	None	18 months
				Oscie H. Kirkland	1 year	None	18 months
				Nash L. Kelley	1 year	None	18 months
				Royal Alexander	6 months	None	3 years
				Lewis Tubb	None	None	1 year
				Ivan Nevill	9 months	None	2 years

Source: Compiled from Commerce Clearing House, Trade Regulation Reports (known popularly as the "Bluebook").
Note: The difference between jail sentence imposed and time to be served is the amount of the sentence suspended.

or operation of a monopoly or trust to be deemed guilty of a felony and imprisoned at hard labor for not less than five years nor more than fifteen years.[15] In 1899 Arkansas Congressman William Terry wanted to amend the Sherman Act so as to provide mandatory imprisonment in criminal cases, and Terry's colleague, Charles Littlefield of Maine, introduced a similar amendment the next year.[16]

It soon became apparent, however, that the makers of laws were more eager to legislate jail terms than the courts were to impose them. One reason for this disparity is the simple fact that in cases involving large corporations it is difficult for a court to pinpoint guilt above the level of those who overtly carry out the antitrust violations. It is not surprising, therefore, that the businessmen who *have* been sentenced to serve time in jail are typically the chief officers of small closely held corporations or low-level and relatively minor officials of large companies.[17] For this reason the jail penalty has not served as an effective deterrent to monopolistic practices.

The inability to determine the true formulators of monopolistic activities within a large corporation is an inherent weakness of any direct penalty aimed at corporate executives. The intent of such an approach was well stated by President Woodrow Wilson in his message to Congress of January 20, 1914, in which he proposed new antitrust legislation:

> [W]e ought to see to it . . . that penalties and punishments should fall not upon business itself, to its confusion and interruption, but upon the individuals who use the instrumentalities of business to do things which public policy and sound business practice condemn. Every act of business is done at the command or upon the initiative of some ascertainable person or group of persons. These should be held individually responsible, and the punishment should fall upon them, not upon the business organization of which they make illegal use.[18]

15. Ibid.
16. Ibid., pp. 514–517.
17. See Comment, "Increasing Community Control Over Corporate Crime— A Problem in the Law of Sanction," *Yale Law Journal* 71 (January 1961): 280, 291.
18. U.S., *Congressional Record,* 63d Cong., 2d Sess., 1914, 51, part 2, 1963.

But as is so often the case in formulating economic legislation, intentions and results have diverged. In the absence of tape recordings of oral communications, the true formulators' instructions to his subordinates can be shrouded in secrecy. Even taped transcripts might prove nothing, since it is not necessary that actual commands be given. The prudent bureaucrat "on the make" in a large corporation can anticipate his superior's wishes without waiting to be told. Those who do play it safe and wait for orders before taking action may find they are expendable. Asking "what would the president of the company want me to do in this situation?" could easily result in a decision either to engage in collusive behavior with the company's rivals or to look the other way when others are violating the law. Robert Paxton, the president of General Electric, admitted that he knew of major violations of the antitrust laws by subordinates but neglected to report his information to Board Chairman Ralph Cordiner. When Senator Estes Kefauver asked for an explanation, Paxton replied that it was not his custom to go about "gossiping." He disliked "tale-bearing," he stated, and he believed that to ask someone "Why didn't you do this, that or some other thing?" is something of a "womanish" characteristic.[19]

In a large organization a subordinate's performance is often judged by a review of his completed actions rather than by an assessment of how well he follows overt commands. For this reason making jail sentences more severe and more frequent would in no way solve the chief problem—the inherent difficulty of pinpointing the actual formulators of antitrust violations.

Congress, recognizing the difficulty of proving the guilt of the top management of the corporations, has from time to time considered amendments to the antitrust laws to deal with this problem. In 1939, for example, a bill was introduced by Senator Joseph C. O'Mahoney to make the mere knowledge of any act of violating the antitrust laws a presumption that the officer of that company authorized and ordered the act. Such person would be subject to fine or imprisonment for not more than one year.[20] In 1961, Lee Loevinger, then assistant attorney

19. Fuller, *The Gentlemen Conspirators,* p. 119.
20. U.S. Congress, Senate, Committee on the Judiciary, *Hearings on S. 2719, To Amend the Antitrust Laws,* 76th Cong., 1st Sess., 1939, p. 2.

general in charge of the Antitrust Division, testified in favor of amending section 14 of the Clayton Act to bring within the scope of the law corporate officials who have knowledge of or "reason to know of an antitrust violation and authority to stop it but fail to do so."[21] The purpose was to authorize sanctions against those who quietly acquiesced in the illegal activities of their subordinates. Under the terms of this proposal, passively condoning violations of the law would be tantamount to engaging in the activity. Although such a law would have made Paxton-type behavior subject to penalty, it would have done little to penalize those who claim no knowledge of the violation. In the same hearings Senator William Proxmire of Wisconsin recognized the ineffectiveness of incarceration as a penalty for antitrust offenses and suggested replacing it with a law that prohibited any corporation officer criminally convicted of violating the antitrust laws from rendering any service to any corporation or receiving compensation from a corporation for a period not exceeding one year. To Proxmire, "a jail sentence is neither [an] appropriate nor an effective deterrent . . . [b]ut requiring a man to leave his job without compensation is a punishment which fits the crime."[22] But this proposal does not overcome the intractable problem of correctly identifying the genuine formulators of policy.

The difficulty of homing in with precision on the real culprits helps explain the high degree of recidivism among the large corporations.[23] Explicitly recognizing the existence of these high rates, Congressman Wright Patman of Texas proposed amending the antitrust laws to provide

21. U.S., Congress, Senate, Committee on the Judiciary, Antitrust Subcommittee, *Headings, Legislation to Strengthen Penalties Under the Antitrust Laws,* 87th Cong., 1st Sess., 1961, p. 14.

22. Ibid., pp. 6–7. Over a decade earlier (on April 10, 1950), Senator Hubert Humphrey of Minnesota introduced S. 3388 in the Eighty-first Congress. This bill would have barred for two to five years the compensation of any person convicted of an antitrust violation by a corporation found guilty in the same proceeding.

23. As Richard Posner has noted, "46 of the 320 corporations that were convicted of a criminal violation of the antitrust laws in cases brought between 1964 and 1968 had previously been convicted, in either a civil or criminal case (or several cases), of the same offense (usually price fixing); and . . . the true percentage of recidivists is undoubtedly higher. Ten of the 46 firms had three or more prior convictions" (Richard A. Posner, "A Statistical Study of Antitrust Enforcement," *Journal of Law & Economics* 13 [October 1970]: 394–395).

for a mandatory jail sentence of not less than thirty days nor more than one year for second and third offenses.[24] Congressman Paul Kilday, also of Texas, stated his support for Patman's proposal, although he was "opposed ordinarily to minimum penalties." As Kilday put it, "For third and fourth offenses, I do not mind putting him away for a little while, at least long enough to take some of those creases out of the tailormade suits they wear."[25] In 1950, Senator Hubert Humphrey wanted to deal with recidivism not by imposing jail sentences but by making any person convicted of a third antitrust offense ineligible to receive compensation from *any* corporation from two to five years. In the 1961 hearings referred to earlier, Lee Loevinger testified in support of legislation to impose a mandatory jail penalty for repeated violations of the antitrust laws. Loevinger stated that such a penalty would add "a very considerable deterrent effect since prison sentences are what individual defendants fear above all."[26]

If Loevinger is right, then surely the fear is out of all proportion to the risk. Considering the virtual nonuse of incarceration as a penalty, it is hard to see why it should be so greatly feared by individual defendants.[27] Making the penalty mandatory probably would only de-

24. U.S., *Congressional Record*, 84th Cong., 1st Sess., 1955, 101, part 3, 3889.
25. Ibid., at p. 3947. Kilday added, "The most effective thing you can do to prevent antitrust violations is to make the penalty against the corporation adequate and make the individuals liable who are sitting in those paneled and air-conditioned directors' offices, or the president's office, cooking up those schemes to violate the antitrust laws. Require them to face the prospect of jail. Then you really put an enforceable provision in it."
26. Senate, *Hearings, Legislation to Strengthen Penalties Under the Antitrust Laws*, p. 69.
27. It should be noted that imprisonment for violating the antitrust laws does not involve precisely the kind of arrangement most people envision, aided by the impressions fostered by motion pictures or television. The prisoners are known as "short timers" and are typically assigned two to a cell. Usually they are issued dungarees and workshirts and are awakened every morning at 6:30 A.M. However, they are given jobs only if they wish them. "They don't have to work if they don't want to," Warden White commented to the Associated Press reporter who covered the incarceration of the electrical equipment conspirators. "The only thing they are responsible for is their cells—and they had better keep them clean." Actually the work which such prisoners usually choose to do probably serves as good occupational therapy. See Fuller, *The Gentlemen Conspirators*, pp. 184–186. Obviously, imposing unpleasantness on the antitrust violator is necessary in order for the penalty to be an effective deterrent. In 1822, the

crease the frequency with which it is imposed. Juries would be loath in such a situation to declare a defendant guilty if they were uncertain whether the leading actors in the antitrust drama had been accurately identified, or were even in court.

Nevertheless, the manipulation of the incarceration penalty remains a highly favored approach among many antitrust enthusiasts. In the debate over the 1974 Antitrust Procedures and Penalties Act, Congressman John Seiberling of Ohio argued that

> if there is any one thing from my own experience that has made the enforcement of the antitrust laws much more meaningful, it was when courts started sentencing corporate executives to jail, because if there is one thing most corporate executives . . . do not like it is having a criminal label attached to them for the rest of their lives and having the reputation of having served time in jail. Believe me that has had a tremendous effect on antitrust compliance within the major businesses of this country.[28]

But Seiberling provided no evidence for his belief, and indeed there is none. In the same debates, Congressman George Danielson disagreed with Seiberling's optimistic appraisal and provided what will doubtless turn out to be a more realistic judgment of the merits of the incarceration feature of the new law:

> the changes brought about by this bill are mere window dressing and could be considered a sham. It means nothing to increase the maximum possible imprisonment for violation of our antitrust laws if one stops to recall that, under the existing laws, the penalty for confinement has rarely been imposed at all.[29]

Reverend Sydney Smith proposed that a prison should be "a place of punishment, from which men recoil with horror—a place of real suffering painful to the memory, terrible to the imagination . . . a place of sorrow and wailing, which should be entered with horror and quitted with earnest resolution never to return to such misery . . ." Sydney Smith, *On the Management of Prisons* (London: Warde Locke and Company, 1822), pp. 226, 232, cited in Gordon Tullock, "Does Punishment Deter Crime?" *The Public Interest* 36 (Summer 1974): 103, 110.

28. U.S., *Congressional Record,* 93d Cong., Nov. 19, 1974, 120, no. 160, H10764.

29. Ibid., H10766.

Nevertheless, there can be no doubt that the deprivation of liberty associated with serving time in jail is not something that most people will face with equanimity. To be assigned to a cell of eighteen by twenty feet, surrounded by stone and steel walls, and provided with only a cot, table, and stool for furnishings and a sink to wash in is an unattractive prospect, especially for someone accustomed to a high salary, well-appointed offices, and living quarters filled with modern conveniences. Perhaps worse, so far as the businessman is concerned, is the humiliation of being handcuffed, fingerprinted, and whisked away from family and friends by a United States marshal. It is a scenario that few would find appealing. But until judges and juries are convinced beyond a reasonable doubt that the well-dressed, wealthy, articulate pillar of the community facing them is in actuality the real instigator and director of a conspiracy to cut back production, rig prices, and rob consumers and taxpayers just as effectively as a common mugger or bank robber, it is unlikely that prison sentences often will be imposed for violations of the antitrust laws.[30] The existence of this penalty in the antitrust arsenal is not a realistic deterrent to corporate criminality.

Structural Relief

The Unique Character of Structural Relief

There is a sense in which the penalty of structural relief stands apart from all of the other antitrust enforcement instruments. The weapons of incarceration, fines, and treble damages could be directed against any imaginable antitrust offense. Structural relief, however, is inextricably tied in with the economic theory that a market's structure is likely to affect competitive performance. This concept is sometimes referred to as the "structure" or "structuralist" theory of antitrust and is widely held

30. The number of times jail sentences are imposed should not be taken as an indicator of the number of times proposals are made for this penalty's implementation. The importance of retaining the jail penalty in the antitrust arsenal and even increasing its severity are continually stressed. In the bill as finally enacted, the Sherman Act was amended to increase the maximum term of imprisonment from one year to three years. Public Law 93–528, 93d Congress, S.782, December 21, 1974, serial 20, p. 3.

by economists, antitrust lawyers, and judges.[31] Where market power is held individually by a single dominant firm or jointly by firms in highly concentrated industries, the structuralist holds that only through dissolution of these dominant firms will the competitive conditions of vigorous rivalry and independent action be assured. The rationale behind structural relief in merger cases is based ultimately on the structuralist theory as well. If a firm is likely to secure market power because of an acquisition, the appropriate remedy, it is alleged, is to divest the acquiring firm of the fruits of its purchase, thereby restoring the market to its previous (and presumably competitive) structure.

Definition of Structural Relief

In common parlance structural relief is called "trust-busting"; the legal nomenclature is dissolution, divorcement, and divestiture. In the following discussion, it will be called DDD. Technically there are differences between dissolution, divorcement, and divestiture.[32] In practice

31. A clear judicial acknowledgment of the structuralist position can be found in the *Brown Shoe* decision: "The Market share which companies may control by merging is one of the most important factors to be considered when determining the probable effects upon competition" (*Brown Shoe Co.* v. *U.S.*, 370 U.S. 294, 343 [1962]).

The structuralist position has been represented in numerous proposals. Perhaps the best known is that of Carl Kaysen and Donald F. Turner. Others who have formulated such recommendations include Henry Simons, Walter Adams, President Johnson's Task Force on Antitrust (the Neal Report), the Ralph Nader Study Group on Antitrust, and Senators Philip Hart and Fred Harris. See Carl Kaysen and Donald F. Turner, *Antitrust Policy: An Economic and Legal Analysis* (Cambridge, Mass.: Harvard University Press, 1959), pp. 266–268; Henry Simons, "A Positive Program for Laissez Faire," in *Economic Policy for a Free Society* (Chicago: University of Chicago Press, 1948), pp. 40–77; Walter Adams, U.S., Senate, Subcommittee on Antitrust and Monopoly, *Hearings, Economic Concentration,* part 1, 88th Cong., 2d Sess., 1964, pp. 353–378; Phil C. Neal et al., *Report of the White House Task Force on Antitrust Policy* (1969), reprinted in *Antitrust Law & Economics Review* 2 (Winter 1968–1969): 11–52; Green et al., *The Closed Enterprise System;* Philip Hart, S. 3832, reprinted in U.S., *Congressional Record,* 92nd Cong., 2d Sess., 1972, 118, part 19, pp. 24925–24935. For Fred Harris's defense of S. 2614, see "The New Populism and Industrial Reform: The Case for a New Antitrust Law," 4 *Antitrust Law & Economics Review* (Summer 1971), pp. 9–46.

32. S. Chesterfield Oppenheim, "Divestiture As A Remedy Under The Federal Antitrust Laws: Economic Background," *George Washington Law Review* 19 (December 1950): 120–131, at 120–121.

the terms are used almost interchangeably to mean the dismemberment of a going firm following an antitrust action. When distinctions are drawn, the term dissolution refers to the termination or dissolving of an association or combination that has violated the antitrust laws. Divestiture means undoing an anticompetitive situation by requiring the sale of some of the defendant firm's assets. Divorcement, the least used of the three terms, represents the result or upshot of a divestiture order.

Many experienced antitrust lawyers cannot draw the precise terminological distinctions between the three terms. Consequently, structural relief, and the "three D's" of antitrust, can best be considered in a generic sense. That is, they will refer to any effort to prevent or undo an antitrust violation through dismembering or reducing the assets of the defendant firm. Most commonly, structural relief is considered appropriate in monopoly and antimerger cases though conceptually it could be used subsequent to any type of antitrust violation.

History of Dissolution, Divorcement, and Divestiture

The railroad baron James Hill is said to have given this evaluation of the government's first effort at accomplishing dissolution: "Two certificates of stock are now issued instead of one; they are printed in different colors, and that is the main difference."[33] This inauspicious beginning was the start of a historical trend. Even ardent supporters of antitrust cannot claim or show many victories at the relief end of an antitrust trial.

George E. Hale constructed the first detailed criticism of defects in the early DDD decrees of the *Standard Oil, American Tobacco, du Pont, International Harvester,* and *Kodak* cases.[34] Earlier these decrees had been criticized by Brandeis, Jones, and others.[35]

33. He was speaking of the decree in *U.S.* v. *Northern Securities Co.,* 193 U.S. 197 (1904), as reported in Matthew Josephson, *The Robber Barons* (New York: Harcourt, Brace, 1962), p. 450.
34. George E. Hale, "Trust Dissolution: Atomizing Business Units of Monopolistic Size," *Columbia Law Review* 40 (April 1940): 615–632, esp. 617–623.
35. Louis D. Brandeis, *United States Tobacco Journal,* August 3, 1912, p. 5, quoted in Reavis Cox, *Competition in the American Tobacco Industry* (New York: Columbia University Press, 1933), p. 39. Elliot Jones, *The Trust Problem in the United States* (New York: Macmillan, 1921).

The heightened antimonopoly activity following World War II did not result in improvements in the relief secured. Walter Adams reviewed the use of structural relief during this period and applied the term "pyrrhic" to the legal victories.[36] Milton S. Goldberg reached the same conclusion in his study of relief secured by consent decree.[37] Jesse Markham refers to the "phantom" victories of antitrust, but Donald Dewey perhaps best summarized the situation with his statement that "it is a commonplace in antitrust work that the government wins the opinions and the defendants win the decrees."[38]

One might presume that undoing mergers would be simpler than untying the assets involved in a monopoly case and that therefore the government's efforts on the merger front would be more successful. But that has not been the case. Two analyses of the Antitrust Division's and Federal Trade Commission's endeavors to secure effective relief in section 7 cases reached much the same conclusion, and the Supreme Court has taken note of this state of affairs.[39]

Kenneth G. Elzinga examined the relief decrees in thirty-nine cases brought under the Celler-Kefauver Act and classified them according to their effectiveness. He found divestiture of the acquired assets or the reestablishment of a viable independent firm to be rare. By his criteria, over three-fourths of the relief decrees in the thirty-nine cases were deficient or unsuccessful. A later study examined a sample of 114 cases brought under section 7 to learn whether divestiture, when ordered, was ever accomplished. In addition, the study evaluated the effectiveness of

36. Walter Adams, "Dissolution, Divorcement, Divestiture: The Pyrrhic Victories of Antitrust," *Indiana Law Journal* 27 (Fall 1951): 1–37.

37. Milton S. Goldberg, *The Consent Decree: Its Formulations and Use,* Michigan State University Graduate School of Business Administration, Occasional Paper No. 8 (East Lansing, Mich.: Bureau of Business and Economic Research, 1962).

38. Jesse W. Markham, "Public Policy and Monopoly: A Dilemma in Remedial Action," *Southern Economic Journal* 16 (April 1950): 413–424, at 422–423; Donald Dewey, "Romance and Realism In Antitrust Policy," *Journal of Political Economy* 63 (April 1955): 93–102, at 93.

39. *Ford Motor Co.* v. *U.S.,* 405 U.S. 562, 582 (1972); Kenneth G. Elzinga, "The Antimerger Law: Pyrrhic Victories?" *Journal of Law & Economics* 12 (April 1969): 43; Malcolm R. Pfunder, Daniel J. Plaine, and Anne M. G. Whittemore, "Compliance with Divestiture Orders Under Section 7 of the Clayton Act: An Analysis of the Relief Obtained," *Antitrust Bulletin* 17 (Spring 1972): 19–180.

those relief efforts. Although the study is not systematic, its general tenor shows a dissatisfaction both with the compliance with section 7 relief decrees and the construction of the decrees themselves.

The economic study of DDD efforts remains a rich field for research. But the consensus so far is that structural relief has been attempted in only a few cases, and it has been performed rather badly in those.

The Legal Theory of Structural Relief

Notwithstanding the dismal track record, the Supreme Court for some time has given the federal courts broad scope in shaping relief remedies: "[Violators] may not reap the benefit of their violations and avoid an undoing of their unlawful project on the plea of hardship and inconvenience."[40] Furthermore, the relief proposals of the enforcement agencies are to be treated favorably by the courts since "once the Government has successfully borne the considerable burden of establishing a violation of the law, all doubts as to the remedy are to be resolved in its favor."[41] Finally, the Court has directed that in those Sherman Act and Clayton Act violations where the nature of the offense is intercorporate control, DDD is the appropriate and logical remedy.[42]

The authority for corporate surgery derives from section 4 of the Sherman Act and section 15 of the Clayton Act. The Federal Trade Commission secures its power from section 11 of the Clayton Act; and, since section 5 violations of the Federal Trade Commission Act can encompass antimerger violations, the commission's broad remedial powers under that act presumably also apply to mergers. In addition, the government enforcement agencies can seek, and have secured, structural relief in the form of consent orders. For a number of reasons, defendants may agree to some form of DDD in lieu of pursuing the antitrust action to its judicial completion. If the two parties to the suit agree upon some form of structural relief, the courts and the com-

---

40. *U.S.* v. *Crescent Amusement Co.*, 323 U.S. 173, 189 (1944); *International Salt Co.* v. *U.S.*, 332 U.S. 392, 400–401 (1947).
41. *U.S.* v. *E. I. du Pont de Nemours & Co.*, 366 U.S. 316, 334 (1961).
42. Ibid., 329–331; *U.S.* v. *Crescent Amusement Co.*; and *U.S.* v. *Grinnell Corp.* 384 U.S. 563, 578, 580 (1966).

mission have been prone to accept without study the consent order.[43] The question of whether private plaintiffs can secure structural relief in an antitrust action has divided legal commentators. In at least one case, a judge did order divestiture in a privately brought antimerger suit, though this decision was reversed upon appeal by the circuit court.[44]

In United States antitrust law, DDD is not seen as a *penalty* for antitrust violations but rather as a *remedy* to be applied in situations where competition cannot be restored otherwise. The Supreme Court has held that, in antitrust civil proceedings, the courts are not "to punish antitrust violators, and relief must not be punitive."[45] In the Department of Justice's celebrated consent decrees with ITT, one of the reasons given as to why the settlement left untouched most of the assets originally listed in the government's complaint was the expressed belief that divestiture of those assets would penalize ITT shareholders.[46] Commentators who are advocates of DDD generally seem to be in accord with this principle. But the legal principle cannot square with economic analysis.

Economic analysis predicts that the exercise of monopoly power yields wealth over and above the competitive return on assets. Presumably these supranormal returns accrue to the owners of the firm, though some of the literature in economics suggests that the firm's managers (if they are distinct from the owners) and possibly the firm's workers may also share in them. If there is a market for the firm's stock (or if the firm has been sold after attaining monopoly power), the monopoly re-

43. For a useful review of this topic, see John J. Flynn, "Consent Decrees In Antitrust Enforcement: Some Thoughts and Proposals," *Iowa Law Review* 53 (April 1968): 983–1019.

44. *ITT* v. *General Telephone & Electronics,* 351 F. Supp. 1153 (1972); *1973 Trade Cases* par. 74,270 (judgment); *1975 Trade Cases* par. 60,291 (reversed).

45. *U.S.* v. *E. I. du Pont de Nemours & Co.,* p. 326. See also *U.S.* v. *Aluminium Ltd.,* 268 F. Supp. 758 (1968). The Federal Trade Commission has also ruled: "We emphasize . . . that the purpose of a Commission order in a restraint of trade case . . . is not punitive, or narrowly or negatively prohibitory" (*Ekco Products Co.,* 65 FTC 1163, 1216 [1964]).

46. Testimony of Richard McLaren, S. Exec. Rep. No. 92–19, 92d Cong., 2d Sess., pt. 4, at 60 (1972). Not all courts seem in harmony with the nonpunitive principle. In *U.S.* v. *ABC Consol. Corp.,* the court held that the prospect of severe financial loss was to provide no escape from compliance with a divestiture order (1968 Trade Cases, par. 73, 621). The Supreme Court on another occasion held that, if necessary, "the Government cannot be denied [divestiture] because economic hardship however severe, may result." (*Gilbertville Trucking Co.* v. *U.S.,* 371 U.S. 115, 130 [1962]).

turns will be capitalized in the stock price (or the sale price) of the firm. Consequently anyone buying shares in a firm already possessing market power (or purchasing the assets of the firm) would earn only a normal rate of return on their investment. This complicates greatly the afore-mentioned principle of applying nonpunitive DDD. To achieve a truly nonpunitive dismemberment of a firm (or industry), as Donald Dewey has argued, is almost a contradiction in terms.[47]

First, if the thorough dissolution of a going firm were not accom-panied by a lowering of its stock prices (or the wealth of current owners and workers), it would suggest that in fact the firm had no monopoly power, which would mean that the original antitrust suit was misguided. Indeed the most accurate test of the magnitude of monopoly power possessed by a firm would be the loss the capital market registers for the value of that firm's stock following its careful dismemberment.[48] If dis-memberment took no toll, it is unlikely there was monopoly power.

A second circumstance in which DDD would not be punitive would occur when the trust is operated by "socially responsible" owners or managers who abstain from exercising their monopoly leverage. If their benevolent policy were known and expected to continue, the capital market would not capitalize these foregone returns and dissolution would involve no financial retribution.[49] But such behavior on the part of businessmen, that is, the existence of so-called good trusts, would certainly attenuate the case for structural relief because structural relief posits a causal link between an industry's structure and its performance. The possible existence of "good trusts" weakens the link by suggesting a conduct test rather than a structural test of anticompetitive perform-ance.

There would, of course, be no penalty visited upon stockholders or

47. Donald Dewey, "Romance and Realism," pp. 99–102. The complications Dewey warned of remain largely unheeded by vigorous proponents of structural relief.

48. By "careful" is meant a dissolving of the monopoly with no adverse im-pact upon the efficiency of the situation, that is, the "new" industry can produce at the same costs as were possible prior to the DDD.

49. The firm would, however, be a likely takeover candidate for any other firm not so temperate in its view toward profit maximization. Moreover, there might be second-order adverse effects following structural relief in the form of private treble damage suits. So long as this possibility exists, the remedy will have punitive impact.

workers of a restructured firm if the DDD "missed" the monopoly power. But such compliance with the Court's doctrine on punitive relief offers no comfort to the proponent of structural relief. There is only one other likely situation where DDD may not appear to impose financial costs upon the firm. In this case, the structural relief occurs fortuitously at a time when the firm's costs have fallen or demand has increased so that the DDD's adverse impact upon the firm, while still real, is not apparent, because it has been offset by events quite distinct from the antitrust action.[50]

The upshot is clear. If structural relief strikes effectively at actual monopoly power, owners or employees or both will suffer a loss in wealth. Stockholders purchasing shares after the original capitalization of the firm's monopoly position will experience the most punitive effects of the DDD, for they will never have shared in the first fruits of the supranormal returns.

The virtual impossibility of nonpunitive structural relief does not necessarily destroy the case for DDD. A legal doctrine could be formulated that permitted punitive dissolution. But such a doctrinal change is unlikely, for it raises the disturbing question of fairness for those who "bought in late." As Dewey speculated, some courts have implicitly understood this problem and herein lies the reason that, historically, the significant examples of structural relief have been associated only with firms where the monopoly power still rested with the promulgators of the monopoly position.[51]

The Administration of DDD

The deliberations over the relief in a prominent monopoly case led Judge Charles Wyzanski to comment on the judicial timidity that historically has been shown toward the use of structural remedies. Referring

50. Dewey offers another example of nonpunitive relief: a case in which the monopoly power destroyed by the DDD "rested upon so precarious a foundation that it had never been capitalized into appreciably higher security prices or incorporated into established employee expectations" ("Romance and Realism," p. 99).

51. The tobacco, petroleum, railroad, and gunpowder cases all involved opportunities for dissolution that, while potentially punitive, would inflict the monetary losses largely upon those individuals who had gained from the monopoly positions. See ibid., p. 101.

specifically to the *Standard Oil, American Tobacco,* and *Alcoa* cases, he said, "To many champions of the anti-trust laws these cases indicate judicial timidity, economic innocence, lack of conviction, or paralysis of resolution."[52] Judicial conservatism toward DDD is not surprising. Trust-busting, after all, is a dramatic remedy and one about which there is very limited knowledge.

The judiciary's caution, moreover, is seldom assuaged by a careful and thorough documentation of the structural alteration proposed by the government. The government's relief proposals, even when including DDD, have seldom been robust.[53] This also is not surprising. An attorney with an enforcement agency can clearly capture certain personal gains by winning an antitrust case. The incentives are there for diligent and thorough labors. However, even if the welfare gains from appropriate DDD were significant, there is little opportunity for them to be captured by agency personnel. The personal incentives are not there for labors as diligent and thorough as those required for trying and winning the case.

Yet judicial temperament or benightedness is not the whole of it. There are mechanical problems as well. One of these is selecting the appropriate assets to be divested (or unscrambling the eggs). Another is finding an appropriate buyer for these assets.

By its very nature, an individual firm has centralized some functions in its managerial structure. Even if the components of multidivision, multiplant firms have substantial operating independence, they will have some of their financial, marketing, and personnel functions carried on from above. The greater the centralization of the firm, both in terms of

52. *U.S.* v. *United Shoe Machinery Corp.,* 110 F. Supp. 295, 348 (1953). Milton Handler described this phenomenon in the *United States Steel* case. "Indeed, one cannot read the opinion in the Steel case without obtaining the firm impression that the Court's apprehension of the adverse effects of dissolution were in part responsible for its doubtful construction and application of the law." See his *A Study of the Construction and Enforcement of the Federal Antitrust Laws,* U.S. TNEC Monograph No. 38 (Washington: U.S. Government Printing Office, 1941), p. 84.

53. In the *United Shoe Machinery* case mentioned in n. 52, Carl Kaysen, who was serving as the law clerk to Judge Wyzanski, wrote that the government's relief presentation was "sketchy, poorly prepared, and failed to come to grips with any of the problems involved." See his *United States* v. *United Shoe Machinery Corporation* (Cambridge, Mass.: Harvard University Press, 1956), p. 343.

its management hierarchy and its physical location, the more difficult is the task of DDD. The most difficult candidate for structural relief is the single-plant monopolist; the easiest candidate is the nonmanaging holding company. Thus, the mechanics of restructuring the electrical power industry under the Public Utility Holding Company Act of 1935, while by no means easy, were simpler than devising structural relief for the single-plant United Shoe Machinery Company.

A structuralist ultimately must face the issue of precisely what assets to sell, because they will vary depending upon the facts of the case. In a world of no administrative costs, the guiding principle would be to separate the firm into as many components as was consistent with retaining economies of scale. But there is little guidance as to the costs involved in correctly deciding what managerial personnel are to go with which firm, the method for decentralizing accounting operations, the rearrangement of the firm's liquid wealth, and the establishment of new worker and supplier relations.

There has been much more experience with these kinds of problems in the administration of the antimerger law. But its history thus far does not provide much encouragement for a program of widespread industrial reorganization. Divestiture under the antimerger law has been particularly hampered by the necessity of deciding what the acquiring firm must relinquish. The general approach, an unfortunate one but perhaps dictated by the law, has been to focus on those assets that were acquired in violation of the law. By the time divestiture is possible, however, these assets may be outdated, altered, or integrated into the parent firm. To divest the firm of them in some cases would be physically impossible or senseless. By way of illustration, when the leading agricultural magazine, *Farm Journal,* acquired its principal rival, *Country Gentlemen,* its gain was essentially a subscription list and the right to solicit the substitution of *Farm Journal* for unexpired *Country Gentlemen* subscriptions.[54] Most of the solicitations were successful, and there remained virtually nothing to divest after a section 7 violation was found. Variations on this theme have occurred in a number of antimerger cases.[55]

---

54. 53 FTC 26, 50 (1956), FTC Docket #6388.
55. See Elzinga, "The Antimerger Law"; and Pfunder, Plaine, and Whittemore, "Compliance with Divestiture Orders."

Another common poser facing a structuralist is that of partial divesti-ure, a problem best illustrated by another example. When the Reed Roller Bit Company acquired American Foundry's American Iron Division, it purchased a company that produced tool joints and drill collars, fluid-end expendable parts, and other products used in the oil drilling business. The only area of direct horizontal overlap between Reed and American Iron was in tool joints and drill collars. Reed argued that, if it had violated section 7, the only divestiture need be this "offend-ng line of commerce." The government trial staff argued that full divestiture of the entire division as acquired was appropriate.

Within the structuralist framework, the Reed position seems correct, and it has become the conventional one in section 7 relief. But the offend-ng line of commerce approach does not work in practice, for partial divestiture is not conducive to reestablishing a viable, independent firm.[56] Carving out the "offending assets" has meant selling them with-out a home or divorcing them from the human capital that would ac-company a full divestiture. Or it has meant parceling out a de minimus bundle of assets whose sale would be unlikely to affect competitive conditions in any market. The eventual result of a partial divestiture order is sometimes no divestiture at all.

Related to the problem of what to unscramble is the problem of "to whom to unscramble." The general result of structural relief is the sale of the excised assets to another ongoing firm (as opposed to the establish-ment of a completely independent firm). It would follow from the structuralist viewpoint that the ideal purchaser is a firm that will operate the divested firm successfully and independently of the original pur-chaser, while not itself representing an anticompetitive acquirer. Such buyers are not readily found. In 1959 the Supreme Court declared Pabst's acquisition of Blatz to be unlawful. In 1974 one could still find, in the brewing trade press, advertisements by Pabst for the sale of the Blatz brewery. Both Elzinga and Pfunder, Plaine, and Whittemore have documented the problems involved in finding any buyer at all, or in

56. When no buyer could be found for the partial divestiture ordered by the court in this case, the order was modified to allow Reed to retain all of the acquisition. See *U.S.* v. *Reed Roller Bit Co.*, 274 F. Supp. 573 (1967) and *1969 Trade Cases*, par. 86, 703.

finding a buyer who could provide viable financial backing for the divested firm. They also found examples of divestiture to a corporate purchaser who did not seem to be an improvement on the original anti competitive acquirer.[57]

Suffice it to say that several factors—the Supreme Court's admonition that structural relief be nonpunitive, the seeming reluctance of both the enforcement agencies and the judiciary to strive for and impose the dismemberment of going firms, the mechanical problems of administer ing relief orders of this type—seem to have combined to destroy any high hopes there may have been for trust-busting as an instrument of antitrust. However, since the chief aim of this book is to examine the efficiency implications of all the antitrust penalties, in a later chapter we shall treat DDD in the same manner as the other weapons, by scrutinizing the costs of achieving whatever benefits might be claimed for it.

Fines

The payment of a sum of money to the state as a penalty for lawbreak ing is one of the oldest and most commonly used methods of inducing compliance with the law. It is not surprising that Congress, in consider ing penalties to be imposed upon the trusts, decided upon a fine as one of the weapons to be placed in the antitrust arsenal. Fines are versatile weapons whose amount can be fixed by law or left to the discretion of the court. In the United States fines cannot be levied without limit, for excessive fines are prohibited under the Eighth Amendment to the Con stitution. However, the magnitude of fines assessed under the antitrust laws has not been such as to test the limits of this constitutional prohibition.

The mechanics of exacting the fine are not precisely the same in all district courts but the normal procedure is for antitrust fines to be paid to the "clerk of the United States district court" with the payments to be made either in cash or by certified check. Credit cards are not ac cepted. The fines are to be paid by both corporate and individual

57. Elzinga, "The Antimerger Law," pp. 61–66; Pfunder, Plaine, and Whitte more, "Compliance with Divestiture Orders," pp. 45–54.

defendants upon assessment. Indeed, in the case of an individual, he or she will generally stand committed until the fine is paid.

Under the original Sherman Act, the maximum fine was $5,000 per count, which could be levied against corporations, individuals, or both. In short order this penalty was seen as rather picayune. Antitrust defendants were not convicted of counts involving such multiples as to make the fine sizable; moreover, judges early showed a propensity not to levy even the full $5,000 per count. The average fine imposed under the $5,000 sanction was less than $2,500 per count.[58] For blue-chip corporations, the result was financial penalties that were de minimus. In 1944 Justice Robert Jackson wrote:

> The antitrust law sanctions are little better than absurd when applied to huge corporations engaged in great enterprise. In the two related Madison Oil cases, 15 of the 17 corporations convicted had combined capital and surplus reported to be $2,833,516,247. The total corporate fines on them were $255,000, making a ratio of fines to corporate capital and surplus of less than one-one hundredth of 1 percent.[59]

Judge Simon Rifkind, prior to imposing fines in the *National Lead* case, admitted that:

> I cannot even go through the formula of looking the defendant in the eye and saying "Is there anything you wish to say before I pronounce sentence?" . . . [A] violation of the antitrust laws which persisted from sometime in the early 1920's to the 1940's with respect to which the criminal liability is discharged by the payment of $5,000 . . . hardly seems . . . to be . . . a penalty which is likely to discourage violations of the antitrust laws . . . but that is a problem for Congress.[60]

This "problem for Congress" remains unresolved. The history of the

58. U.S., Congress, House, *Hearings of Subcommittee To Study Increasing Criminal Penalties Under the Sherman Antitrust Act* (*H.R. 2237*), 83rd Cong., 2d Sess., 1954, p. 3 (hereafter cited as *1954 Hearings*).

59. *U.S.* v. *South-Eastern Underwriters Association,* 322 U.S. 533, 591 (1944).

60. *U.S.* v. *National Lead,* Cr. 114–115 (S.D.N.Y.) cited in *1954 Hearings,* p. 3.

Sherman Act fine has been a recital of attempts to increase the penalty to an apposite level.[61]

As early as 1900, a scant decade after the passage of the Sherman Act, a House committee reported that the Sherman Act penalties were unacceptably low.[62] When the Clayton Act was being deliberated, this sentiment was again expressed. At the conclusion of the Temporary National Economic Committee's study, the most massive investigation of the monopoly problem ever undertaken by the Congress, once again the recommendation was made that the fine be increased.[63] Over the years Congress considered bills to augment the fine at least a dozen times, but not until 1955 did both houses of the Congress pass such a bill, increasing the financial penalty tenfold to a maximum of $50,000.[64]

However, efforts to secure even a small amount of monopoly power particularly if expected to pay off for a year or more, were not to be deterred by a $50,000 penalty, especially when discounted by a probability of detection and conviction of less than one. For example, in the most prominent price-fixing case since the 1955 amendment (the electrical equipment conspiracy), the average fine imposed upon each corporate defendant was only $16,550. Furthermore, the maximum fine of $50,000 was imposed but once in the more than 150 sentences handed down.[65] The General Electric Company alone was found guilty of nineteen counts, for an aggregate fine of $437,500. This amount was less than 0.001 of the company's total profit and less than 0.003 of its net profit for a single year.[66] Congressman Wright Patman was fond of saying that a Sherman Act fine was less than a large company paid a celebrity for a single television broadcast. Clabault and Burton calculated

61. For a useful outline of the legislative efforts, see U.S., Congress, House Select Committee on Small Business, *Congress and the Monopoly Problem,* 80th Cong., 2d Sess., 1966.

62. U.S. Congress, House, *Protection of Trade and Commerce Against Unlawful Restraints and Monopolies,* 56th Cong., 1st Sess., 1900, Rept 1506, p. 2

63. The TNEC final report advised raising the fine to at least $50,000. See U.S., Congress, Temporary National Economic Committee, *Final Report and Recommendations,* 77th Cong., 1st. Sess., 1941, p. 40.

64. 26 Stat. 209, Public Law No. 190, 51st Cong.

65. "Increasing Community Control Over Corporate Crime," p. 287.

66. The year was 1960. Taken from testimony of Assistant Attorney General Lee Loevinger, Senate, *Hearings, Legislation To Strengthen Penalties Under the Antitrust Laws,* p. 12.

Table 2. Criminal Sanctions—Fines

Period n Which Case Was nstituted	Total Criminal Convictions	Number of Cases in Which Fine Was Imposed	Aggregate Amount of Fines Imposed in Period	Average Fine per Case
390–1894	0	0		
395–1899	0	0		
900–1904	1	1	1,000	1,000
905–1909	11	10	218,875	21,876
910–1914	21	19	400,090	21,057
915–1919	13	13	145,857	11,220
920–1924	15	13	764,850	58,835
925–1929	14	12	796,510	66,376
930–1934	8	7	142,444	20,349
935–1939	19	17	882,914	51,936
940–1944	123	123	6,319,506	51,378
945–1949	50	50	1,790,123	35,802
950–1954	65	64	1,197,537	18,711
955–1959	86	86	4,306,375	50,074
960–1964	64	62	7,846,552	126,557
965–1969	46	46	5,364,633	116,622

SOURCE: Richard A. Posner, "A Statistical Study of Antitrust Enforcement," Journal of Law and Economics 13 (October 1970): 392.
NOTE: Average fine per case is calculated by dividing aggregate amount of fines by number of cases.

that in the first thirteen years under the $50,000 provision 897 corporations were fined a total of $12,094,667. This meant the average corporate fine was only $13,483. The average fine levied upon individuals was even more miniscule: slightly over $3,000.[67] Richard A. Posner has calculated the average fine *per case* for the 1890–1969 period.[68] Table 2 is taken from Posner's statistical compilations. This table corroborates the small size of the fine and also indicates that judges did not even approach full use of the tenfold increase in the fine available to them after 1955.

These magnitudes have led antitrust observers of various persuasions to recommend an elevation in the fine. For example, the antitrust task

67. Clabault and Burton, *Sherman Act Indictments,* p. 42.
68. Posner, "A Statistical Study of Antitrust Enforcement," pp. 365, 392.

force assembled by President Nixon supported such an increase, as did the Ralph Nader study group on the antitrust laws.[69] Attorney General William Saxbe proposed a $500,000 fine on antitrust violators, a figure that was subsequently doubled in a recommendation sent to Congress by President Ford.[70] No testimony recommending a decrease in the antitrust fines has ever been offered, although Charles E. Wilson perhaps came closest in his testimony as president of the General Electric Company. Wilson was asked in 1949 whether he thought the fine was adequate to deter antitrust wrongdoing. He replied that he had not thought through the question of whether the fine needed to be higher than $5,000.[71] Only one piece of legislation has called for a reduction in the fine. This bill was proposed in the Eighty-fifth Congress and would have reduced the fine from $50,000 to the original $5,000.[72]

The precise manner in which the fine should be increased has been the subject of disagreement among those proposing this change. There are three options: increase the absolute amount of the fine; impose a variable or graduated fine; or direct a higher fine specifically at those business managers responsible for the antitrust violation.

The first approach is exemplified by the proposed legislation of Senators Philip Hart and Roman Hruska, which sought to increase the Sherman Act penalty to $500,000. This legislation dated back to 1961 and 1962 when hearings were held before the Senate Antitrust and Monopoly Subcommittee on the need for additional deterrent proposals and the proposal had received the support of the Department of Justice, the Council of Economic Advisers, and the American Bar Association.[73]

During legislative debates on raising the Sherman Act penalty, however, Congressman Wright Patman objected to a simple increase in the

69. Cf. Report Of The Task Force On Productivity And Competition, reprinted in *Antitrust Law & Economics Review* 2 (Spring 1969): 13, 33, statement of George J. Stigler; Mark J. Green, *The Closed Enterprise System*, p. 175.

70. "Saxbe Asks Jail For Antitrust, Tax Violators," *Washington Post*, October 5, 1974, p. A3; "Ford Outdoes Justice Dept. In Antitrust Fine Proposal," *Washington Post*, October 10, 1974, p. A11.

71. U.S. Congress House, Committee on the Judiciary, *Hearings, Study of Monopoly Power*, 81st Cong., 1st Sess., Part 2-B, 1949.

72. H.R. 12786, 85th Cong.

73. U.S. Congress, Senate, Committee on the Judiciary, *Hearings, Increasing Sherman Act Criminal Penalties*, 91st Cong., 2d Sess., 1970.

THE PUBLIC ACTION PENALTIES

ine. He argued that a single fine, whatever the dollar figure, would have disproportionate deterrent effects upon different size firms.[74] He proposed a fine of not less than 5 percent and not more than 10 percent of the corporation's assets as of the date on which the charge of violation was filed.[75] Another antitrust proponent on Capitol Hill who favored a graduated penalty was Estes Kefauver. In an address before the American Economic Association, he recommended that the fine levied on antitrust violators be in a fixed ratio to the firm's invested capital.[76] The Nader study group on the antitrust laws also recommended a proportional fine, based on the corporation's sales.[77] In a similar vein, Kenneth W. Dam has suggested that the fine be made proportional to the gain to the corporation from the antitrust violation. In this way small corporations presumably would not be subject to Brobdingnagian fines, while large corporations would be eligible for sizable financial penalties.[78]

The earliest reference in support of a true graduated fine was recorded in 1939 when Senator Joseph C. O'Mahoney proposed a bill in which any corporation that violated the antitrust laws would be made liable, in a civil action brought by the United States, to forfeit an amount equal to twice its total net income during the entire time of the antitrust violation.[79]

Those urging an increase in the fine have also suggested that the penalty be levied on the management directly responsible for the antitrust violation. In this way a fine need not be gargantuan to deter even

74. "If you fine a $500,000 corporation $50,000, you are fining that corporation 10 percent of its assets. If you fine a million dollar corporation $50,000, you are fining that corporation 5 percent of its assets. I am not objecting to it. That is a good deterrent to put the fear of the Lord in the little fellow, but why stop here? Why not run that 5 percent clear across the board?

"The 5 percent, therefore, would apply not only to the little man but also to the billionaire corporation. That is the type of amendment I favor." U.S. *Congressional Record,* 84th Cong., 1st Sess., 1955, 101, part 3, 3941–3942.

75. U.S. *Congressional Record,* 84th Cong., 1st Sess., 1955, 101, part 3, 3888.

76. Estes Kefauver, "Needed Changes In Legislation," *American Economic Review* (Proceedings) 38 (May 1948): 182–202.

77. Green, *The Closed Enterprise System,* p. 175.

78. Testimony of Kenneth W. Dam, Senate, *Hearings, Increasing Sherman Act Criminal Penalties,* p. 27.

79. U.S., Congress, Senate, *Hearings on S. 2719, To Amend The Antitrust Laws,* 76th Cong., 1st Sess., 1939, p. 16.

the largest corporation since the fine will come from private individual
rather than the corporate coffers. As mentioned in the discussion of in
carceration, this sentiment was first expressed in the debates on th
Clayton Act and section 14 of that act provides for a possible fine o
up to $5,000 on any officer, director, or agent of the corporate of
fender.[80] This section has proved of no value as a deterrent becaus
judges have been reluctant to impose even the puny penalty provided

As a result, amendments to section 14 have been introduced to in
crease the expected value of the fine, either by raising the penalty
removing some of the judiciary's discretion in assigning paltry fines
compelling the involvement of all corporate officials who ratify antitrus
violations, or all of these. It should be recalled that Senator O'Mahoney'
1939 proposed amendment to section 14 would consider as a violato
of the antitrust laws any corporate official or director who would hav
knowledge of any antitrust violation since, by virtue of this knowledge
he "shall be presumed to have authorized, ordered, or caused such ac
. . ."[81] The penalty for such knowledge and presumed ratification of th
violation was a fine not exceeding $5,000 plus a sum equal to twic
the total compensation of the corporate employee or director. This
Senator O'Mahoney thought, loosely tied the fine to the size of th
offense and also gave the corporate officials an incentive not only t
disapprove antitrust violations but to thwart them actively within th
corporation as well.

There have been other variations on this theme. Congressman Patma
has supported a simple raising of the fine on individuals with a floor c
$5,000 and a ceiling of $50,000 for the first offense, increasing t
$7,500 and $75,000 respectively for a second or third offense.[82] Le
Loevinger, when head of the Antitrust Division, testified in support c
a Senate bill that would have brought within the scope of the antitrus
laws all corporate officials who ratify antitrust violations.[83] Thus, whil
any corporate employee who participated in a price-fixing scheme woul
be eligible for punishment under the Sherman Act, this bill (and othe

80. Section 14, 38 Stat. 730; Public Law No. 212, 63d Cong. (1914).
81. Senate, *Hearings To Amend The Antitrust Laws (S. 2719)*, p. 2.
82. U.S., *Congressional Record*, 84th Cong., 1st Sess., 1955, 101, part 3, 388
83. See statement of Lee Loevinger and generally Senate, *Hearings, Legisl
tion To Strengthen Penalties Under The Antitrust Laws*, pp. 14–15.

bills like it) would also fine any corporate officials who authorize, sanction, or acquiesce in such violations. The proposed sanctions imposed upon such businessmen included not only higher fines and salary forfeiture but also temporary loss of employment and mandatory jail sentences.

In the final version of the Antitrust Procedures and Penalties Act, which was signed by the president in December 1974, the maximum corporation fine was increased to $1 million and the severity of a violation was changed from a misdemeanor to a felony. The Senate version of the bill had provided maximum fines of $500,000 for corporations, but the president had recommended a $1 million fine in his economic message of October 8, 1974. The presidential proposal was a surprise since the Department of Justice had supported a $500,000 limit. For example, Bruce D. Wilson, deputy assistant attorney general of the Antitrust Division, testified that the Justice Department would not favor increasing the penalty above $500,000 on the grounds that this penalty along with the additional deterrent of treble damage actions would hopefully be adequate.[84] However, Thomas E. Kauper, the head of the Antitrust Division, had personally favored the $1 million fine despite Attorney General Saxbe's proposal for a $500,000 upper limit.[85]

The viability of the fine as an antitrust weapon can be easily summarized. As presently constituted, it is an ineffectual deterrent to anticompetitive activity. In an expected value sense, its size is small, even under the new provisions of the Antitrust Procedures and Penalties Act. The new law has raised the ceiling on fines but has not set a floor under them. The size of the fine ultimately imposed still is at the discretion of the trial court. And, as Deputy Assistant Attorney General Walker B. Comegys noted, from 1967 to 1970, in cases where sentencing occurred, the Department of Justice itself had recommended the maximum fine only 27 percent of the time.[86] At that time, of course, the fine was

84. U.S., Congress, House, Committee on the Judiciary, Subcommittee on Monopolies and Commercial Law, *Hearings, Consent Decree Bills,* 93d Cong., 1st Sess., 1973, p. 75.
85. "Ford Outdoes Justice Dept. in Antitrust Fine Proposal," p. A11.
86. Statement of Walker B. Comegys before the Senate Judiciary Subcommittee on Antitrust and Monopoly, March 4, 1970, as cited in House, *Hearings, Consent Decree Bills,* p. 92.

only $50,000 per count. When the risk attitudes of American business-men are considered, a nonmandatory fine becomes even less potent. A later chapter will show, however, that the fine is the weapon with the most potential for deterring antitrust violations because of its unusual properties, properties that are not shared by any other instruments in the antitrust arsenal.

4

THE PRIVATE ACTION PENALTY:
TREBLE DAMAGES

Treble Damages in Historical Context

In 1623 a statute concerning monopolies was passed in Parliament. It provided that an individual, financially injured in his business or property by a restraint of trade, could bring suit and, if successful, collect treble the amount of his damages from the perpetrator of the anticompetitive activity.[1] This statute eventually established the pattern for the most intricate and factious of all the American antitrust penalties, that of treble damages, which Congress included in the Sherman Act. The pertinent section of that act provided:

> Any person who shall be injured in his business or property . . . by reason of anything forbidden . . . by this act, may sue therefore . . . , without respect to the amount in controversy, and shall recover threefold the damages by him sustained, and the costs of suit, including a reasonable attorney's fee.[2]

Section 7 of the Sherman Act, now superseded by section 4 of the Clayton Act, enables private persons not only to bring antitrust suits but also to seek treble damages for financial injury suffered as a result of the antitrust violation.[3]

1. "An act concerning monopolies and dispensations with penal laws and forfeitures thereof," 21 Jac. I, c. 3 (1623).
2. Act of July 2, 1890, Ch. 647, § 7, 26 Stat. 210.
3. Section 4 of the Clayton Act now provides for the enactment of treble damage suits under the antitrust laws. A pending government antitrust action tolls the four-year statute of limitations on private damage suits until one year after completion of the government action. 38 Stat. 731 (1914), 15 U.S.C. § 15.

In constructing this particular instrument, Congress had to settle three distinct issues. The first issue was the role the private sector was to have in filing and pursuing antitrust suits (as opposed to seeking damages only). The second was the amount of damages for which injured persons were to be eligible. The third was the question of who would bear the legal costs involved in this private enforcement approach to antitrust. It will be convenient to take the issue of the amount of damages first since there was little debate on it.

The Amount of Damages

Double damages was the initial multiple proposed by Senator Sherman.[4] Later he changed his mind and suggested that only "full consideration" (presumably single damages) be restored to injured private parties. Exactly why he reverted to double damages in his final draft is not known.[5] Senator Sherman's draft, along with a number of amendments, was sent to the Senate's Judiciary Committee for a complete overhaul. There Senator George Hoar of Massachusetts composed what became section 7 of the Sherman Act. Though the first sections of the act represented a codification of the English common law, Hoar took his cue for section 7 from the English statute of monopolies. While it is known that the senator considered double damages insufficient, there is no record of the committee's deliberations that reveals if multiples higher than three were considered.[6] The Biblical precedent would suggest a fourfold (if not sevenfold) multiplication.[7]

There have been sporadic attempts to reduce the size of the multiplier. Only eight years after the Sherman Act's passage, Congressman

4. S. 3445 (August 14, 1888), U.S., *Congressional Record,* 50th Cong., 1st Sess., 1888, 19, part 8, 7513.

5. Sec. 2, S. 1 (January 14, 1890), U.S., Congress, Senate, I, *Bills and Debates in Congress Relating to Trusts,* 57th Cong., 1st Sess., 1903, p. 71. See also U.S., *Congressional Record,* 51st Cong., 1st Sess., 1889, 21, part 2, 1765–1768.

6. See George F. Edmunds, "The Interstate Trust and Commerce Act of 1890," *The North American Review* 194 (December 1911): 801, as cited in U.S., Congress, House, Committee on the Judiciary, *Hearings, Discretionary Treble Damages In Private Antitrust Suits,* 83rd Cong., 1st Sess., 1954, p. 54 (hereafter cited as *Hearings on H.R. 4597*).

7. II Samuel 12:1–6; Proverbs 6:30–31.

William Greene, a Populist from Nebraska, proposed diminishing the damage multiple to twofold.[8] The proposal that was perhaps given the most serious consideration was that of Congressman William Hepburn, of the Committee on Interstate Commerce. His 1908 proposal, which was the outgrowth of the prominent Chicago conference on the trust problem, would have limited private plaintiffs to single damages.[9] Much later, in 1953, hearings were held on Congressman Chauncey Reed's bill. That bill would have enabled the courts, at their discretion, to reduce the damage award below the trebled amount.[10] Congressman Francis E. Walter of Pennsylvania became a rather persistent proponent of similar legislation but his enthusiasm for it was kept in check by the House Judiciary Committee's propensity to keep his bill in committee.[11] The Attorney General's National Committee to Study the Antitrust Laws also argued that in some instances the damage multiple should be lowered to Senator Sherman's original double damages.[12]

There have been no proposals to have the damages multiplied by a figure larger than three. However, there have been numerous endeavors to indirectly accomplish the same purpose by enlarging the potential multiplicand. Such measures have included easing the burden of proof of damages, enlarging the class of potential plaintiffs, lengthening the statute of limitations on such suits, facilitating the assembling of potential plaintiffs, and permitting consent decrees and pleas of *nolo contendere* to serve as prima facie evidence of guilt in private damage suits. Any of these would increase the expected value of a treble damage payment, thereby having the same effect as raising the multiplier.

8. Hans B. Thorelli, *The Federal Antitrust Policy: Origination of an American Tradition* (Baltimore: Johns Hopkins Press, 1955), pp. 509–510. Greene's bill also would have enlarged the scope of private damage suits.

9. See William Letwin, *Law and Economic Policy in America: The Evolution of the Sherman Antitrust Act* (New York: Random House, 1965), pp. 248–249.

10. See *Hearings on H.R. 4597.*

11. For example see H.R. 4958, 84th Cong., March 15, 1955; H.R. 978, 85th Cong., March 3, 1957; H.R. 1184, 86th Cong., January 7, 1959; H.R. 190, 87th Cong., January 3, 1961.

12. See U.S., Justice Department, *Report of the Attorney General's National Committee to Study Antitrust Laws*, 1955, p. 379. A more recent proponent of selectively reducing the treble damage award is Kenneth W. Dam. See his testimony on S. 3036, U.S., Congress, Senate, Committee on the Judiciary, *Hearings, Increasing Sherman Act Penalties*, 91st Cong., 2d Sess., 1970, p. 25.

The efforts of Congress and the courts to alter the multiplicand have far exceeded those to change the multiplier, both in terms of ingenuity shown and resources exhausted.

The Role of the Private Sector

The issue as to whether Congress intended private actions to be the primary tool for deterring anticompetitive activity or instead meant it to be simply a device enabling the recompensing of injured parties is by no means merely semantic. For if the appropriate purpose of the private treble damage suit is deterrence, the litigation of private suits should then be encouraged in the courts and the awarding of damages becomes paramount. Damages should be awarded to *someone* (so that a deterrent effect is manifested), even if that party is not the one specifically injured by the antitrust violation. However, if compensation is the goal, then those not injured by anticompetitive activity have no business in court (even if their suit attacks a bona fide antitrust violation), and a greater role for the government as the agent of enforcement is logical.

Any stark portrayal of *the* congressional intent concerning Sherman Act enforcement should be given the same credibility today ascribed to the findings of the haruspex. For as Walton Hamilton put it, "the bill which was ardously debated [Sherman's bill] was never passed, and . . . the bill which was passed [the Judiciary Committee's] was never really discussed."[13] Oddly, this analysis did not restrain Hamilton from bluntly ascribing to Congress the desire to "make the suit for triple damages the main instrument for enforcing the act." He argued that the legislators were then such believers in the orthodox creed of laissez-faire that they wanted to make the Sherman Act almost self-enforcing.[14] Thorelli subscribes to much this same view.[15] Further support for this theory comes from the simple fact that Congress originally provided no funds specific

13. Walton Hamilton, *Antitrust in Action,* TNEC Monograph No. 16, (1940), p. 10.

14. Testimony of Walton Hamilton, U.S., Congress, House, Committee on the Judiciary, *Hearings, Study of Monopoly Power,* 81st Cong., 1st Sess., part 1, 1949, p. 287.

15. Thorelli, *Federal Antitrust Policy,* pp. 229, 558.

to Sherman Act enforcement. The first appropriation for antitrust work at the Department of Justice was not made until 1903.

However, Congress actually perceived only a modest role for reparations-induced antitrust enforcement. There is, in fact, little explicit expression of the Hamilton-Thorelli viewpoint in the congressional debates. The specific origins and evils of the trusts, their relationship to tariffs, the sincerity of the Republican's antitrust endeavors, and the possible unconstitutionality of antitrust legislation dominated the discussion. Furthermore, when the private damage provision was debated, a number of ardent antitrusters in the Senate expressed the view that private parties would not be able to afford such legal battles, especially in the federal courts.[16] In addition, men as committed to laissez-faire as Hamilton depicts them as being, would be unlikely to envisage or welcome a massive influx of antitrust regulation by *any* sector. The fact that no appropriation was given for public enforcement also squares with the thesis, usually associated with Clark and Fainsod and Gordon, that Congress (or at least many of its members) did not want intensive antitrust enforcement, public or private.[17]

Even the lack of a specific appropriation does not necessarily mean antitrust proponents expected to rely solely on private enforcement. The policing of trusts was assigned to the attorney general and the various district attorneys. Some members of Congress may have thought (incorrectly, to be sure) that the district attorneys, being "in the field," would be vigilant detectors of anticompetitive activity. Finally, as Thorelli concedes, some congressmen may have decided the mere passage of a prohibitory statute would induce compliance with the law without significant enforcement efforts by either the government or private parties.

To the slight extent one can generalize about the wishes of Congress,

---

16. See the *Congressional Record* containing the debates of this period. Also useful is "The History of the Private Action For Treble Damages Under the Antitrust Laws," prepared by Motion Picture Association of America, reprinted in *Hearings on H.R. 4597,* pp. 45–58.

17. John D. Clark, *The Federal Trust Policy* (Baltimore: Johns Hopkins Press, 1931), pp. 27–37, 52–53; Merle Fainsod and Lincoln Gordon, *Government and the American Economy* (New York: Norton, 1941), pp. 450–452.

two facts now seem incontrovertible. First, if Congress expected substantial enforcement efforts from the private sector, it was sadly mistaken. During the first fifty years of Sherman Act enforcement only 175 such suits were filed; of these, plaintiffs were successful in only 13.[18] Second, if Congress originally had hoped to make the antitrust laws self-enforcing, it was disabused of this notion by the time the 1914 antitrust legislation was passed. Both the Federal Trade Commission Act and the Clayton Act implied a greater weight was to be placed on public enforcement.[19] The former established a government agency that was to police anticompetitive activity. Section 5(a) of the Clayton Act provided:

> A final judgment or decree . . . rendered in any . . . proceeding brought by . . . the United States under the antitrust laws to the effect that the defendant has violated such laws shall be prima facie evidence against such defendant in any action . . . brought by any other party . . .

This section thus enabled private parties to free ride, taking advantage of government enforcement antitrust victories in their efforts to seek reparations. This provision emphasizes the importance of the compensation aspect of treble damage suits, and, ipso facto, recognizes the difficulties of the private sector in single-handedly ferreting out, litigating against, and thereby deterring monopolistic activity.

The attempts that have been made to influence congressional views on reparations-induced enforcement are mere skirmishes compared to the action on the judicial front, for there is the battleground upon which the ultimate role of this antitrust penalty is determined. The battle thus far has shown casualties on both sides and encompasses legal conflicts beyond the scope of this chapter. A skeletal account of the litigation of treble damage suits will be given here to provide a jumping-off point for

18. Note, "Proof Requirements in Anti-Trust Suits: The Obstacles to Treble Damage Recovery," *University of Chicago Law Review* 18 (Autumn 1950): 130, 138.

19. The primary impetus for additional public enforcement was not the lackluster performance of private suits as such but rather the difficulties the Sherman Act faced in the courts. In particular, the Supreme Court's handling of cases against the sugar, petroleum, and tobacco trusts persuaded Congress that an administrative approach to antitrust enforcement was apposite.

the rather detailed economic analysis of this instrument that will follow.[20]

Simplified, the mechanics of a private treble damage suit involve: (1) the proof of an antitrust violation by the defendant; (2) the proof that the plaintiff has been damaged as a result of the violation; and (3) the proof of the extent of the damages. Private plaintiffs have been assisted in overcoming the first hurdle by section 5 of the Clayton Act. According to the conventional pattern, the private party enters after a successful government suit. Although this pattern is still common, especially for the more serious violations like price fixing, in recent years the private antitrust bar has shown a greater propensity to tackle the proof of violation as well.

To undertake either of the first two elements of a private antitrust action, the plaintiff must demonstrate standing to sue. Individuals, business enterprises (even potential business enterprises), municipalities, and states have been granted standing to sue; shareholders, unions, creditors, and third parties doing business with the defendant generally have been found not to have standing. Since the economic theory of standing to sue will be discussed later, at this point let it be said that this issue remains one of the more opaque in antitrust law. Plaintiffs' efforts to show that they have been within the required "target area" and sustained "direct injury" are done in a milieu of case law that has not attained high analytical rigor or predictability.[21] To be sure, the entire concept of standing is not an easy one. It involves drawing a line somewhere in the cause-effect relationships of an interdependent economy.

The Supreme Court has established that a complainant must carefully prove both a loss of wealth *and* the connection between this wealth loss

---

20. For a detailed exposition of the legal issues, see E. Compton Timberlake, *Federal Treble Damage Antitrust Actions* (Mundelein, Ill.: Callaghan and Co., 1965). For a summary of the case law, see American Bar Association, *Antitrust Developments 1955–1968* (Chicago: American Bar Association, 1968) and the pocket supplement.

21. "Private antitrust actions are founded upon injuries that would proximately or directly result from the commission of the ... [antitrust violation] ... and recovery and damages ... are available only to those who have been directly or proximately injured by the ... violation and are withheld from those who seek the windfall of treble damages because of incidental harm" *(Fiumara v. Texaco, Inc.,* 204 F. Supp. 544, 547 [1962], aff'd 310 F. 2d 737 [1962]).

and the antitrust violation.[22] The law makes a distinction between proving the *fact* of damage and proving the *amount* of damage, a distinction that is not logically obvious in economic analysis. Presumably, however, when the more stringent test of fact of damage has been made, the burden upon the plaintiff to prove the amount of damages is much lighter.[23]

Conceptually, showing the amount of injury requires demonstrating the wealth position of the plaintiff after the antitrust violation and projecting what this position would have been in the absence of the violation. Since economic events cannot be replayed under various "as if" conditions, determining damages involves estimation. There are two broad categories of losses: (1) those resulting from overcharges by firms with market power; and (2) those due to a loss of sales or profits owing to such anticompetitive exclusionary techniques as boycotts, foreclosures, tying arrangements, and the like. Three general estimation techniques have met with judicial favor. The most obvious is the "before and after" method. An example would be the technique used by a businessman who, having purchased from a cartel, argues that his damages were equal to the difference between the price he paid during the cartel's existence and the price paid prior to the formation of the cartel (when the market was presumably competitive), all multiplied by the quantity of the product purchased during the life of the cartel.[24] Another tactic is that of the "yardstick," which involves finding a firm or person comparable in every way to the plaintiff—except that the yardstick party did not incur the damages of the instant antitrust violation. A comparison of the yardstick's financial performance with that of the plaintiff provides an estimate of the plaintiff's injury.[25] In the third approach, third party

---

22. *Story Parchment* v. *Paterson Parchment Paper Co.,* 282 U.S. 555 (1931).

23. *Atlas Building Products Co.* v. *Diamond Block & Gravel Co.,* 269 F. 2d 950 (1959), cert. denied, 363 U.S. 843 (1960). See also *Bigelow* v. *RKO Radio Pictures, Inc.,* 327 U.S. 251 (1946). Richard Posner attributes the significant increase in the filing of treble damage suits to the substantial lowering of the third hurdle as a result of the latter suit. See Posner, "A Statistical Study of Antitrust Enforcement," *Journal of Law & Economics* 13 (October 1970): 374.

24. See cases cited at pp. 317–328 in Timberlake, *Federal Treble Damage Antitrust Actions.*

25. See the cases cited at pp. 328–333 in ibid.

sources, generally the testimony of experts, are used to estimate financial injury.[26]

Private treble damage plaintiffs have been assisted by their ability to present their cases before only one judge where all plaintiffs suffered from the same violation. The Judicial Panel on Multidistrict Litigation's *Manual for Complex and Multidistrict Litigation* describes the procedures (which grew out of the electrical equipment cases) for coordinating lawsuits. In addition, rule 23 of the Federal Rules of Civil Procedure has facilitated the filing of complaints as class actions. It has enabled individuals who separately would not find a suit worthwhile, or even feasible, to band together as a class, pool evidence, avoid duplication costs, and collectively sue for what in some cases have been gargantuan amounts.

Defendants may try to use any of several obvious methods to avoid losing treble damage actions: attempting to show there was no antitrust violation; claiming that a successful government action bears no relation to the private plaintiffs charges; arguing that the plaintiff does not have standing to sue or was not directly in the "target area"; or claiming that plaintiff's proof of damages is too speculative to enable judgment. Defendants may argue that the plaintiff himself has "unclean hands" because of antitrust violations on his part or seek to argue *in pari delicto* (at equal fault), alleging that the plaintiff is guilty of the same antitrust violation for which he seeks damages. The latter two defenses are of little use today. The other defense of note is that of "passing on." This term refers not to a defense based on death but rather to an alleged lack of injury to the plaintiff because any overcharges or damages suffered have been passed on to the plaintiff's customers. The courts take a very dim view of this defense. With the possible exception of unusual situations (such as a cost-plus contract), the Supreme Court has held that a plaintiff is eligible for damages even if the overcharge has been passed on in the form of higher prices.[27] In this way, the Court seeks to facilitate private actions and to prevent antitrust violators from escaping

26. Ibid., p. 333.
27. *Hanover Shoe Machinery Inc.* v. *United Shoe Machinery Corp.*, 392 U.S. 481 (1969).

damage payments because those ultimately injured (like the final consumer) are not viable candidates as plaintiffs in damage suits.

Legal Fees and Private Actions

Section 4 of the Clayton Act provides that successful plaintiffs are to be awarded "reasonable attorney's fees" from defendants, in addition to the treble damage payment. Since the legal system of the United States generally does not provide for the successful litigant to receive payment for legal expenses from the losing party, this provision is somewhat peculiar to the institution of antitrust. Note that the award process is not symmetrical; that is, unsuccessful plaintiffs need not pay the legal expenses incurred by defendants. Therefore the net effect of this provision is to add even more to the incentive to bring private actions.

The purpose of the "reasonableness" criterion in section 4 is, of course, to protect unsuccessful defendants from being confronted with unreasonable bills from opposing counsel. That amount which constitutes a reasonable fee is ultimately at the court's discretion. In the past, courts have approved fees ranging from a few hundred dollars to millions of dollars and from at least 14 percent to 4308 percent of the single damages.[28] On an hourly basis, reasonable legal fees have varied from at least $4.37 to $128.00 per hour.[29]

Judges purportedly weigh a variety of factors in assessing a reasonable fee. These factors include the time expended by the plaintiff's counsel, the reputation and expertise of the lawyers, the nature and difficulty of the case, the amount of recovery, and, in at least one case, a guideline of avoiding amounts that would "shock the conscience."[30] The vagaries

28. Kevin F. Kelly, "Comment, Attorney's Fees in Individual and Class Action Antitrust Litigation," *California Law Review* 60 (November 1972): 1656, 1679–1782.

29. Ibid., p. 1666. The figures are based on a subsample of the seventeen cases in which hourly rates could be calculated, drawn from the sample of forty-seven cases studied.

30. *Milwaukee Towne Corp.* v. *Loew's Inc.,* 190 F. 2d 561, 569–571 (1951). In this case an appellate court reduced the attorney's fee from $225,000 to $75,000 on the grounds that the original fees would "equal the total annual salary received by all the members of the Supreme Court." See also *Twentieth Century-Fox Film Corp.* v. *Brookside Theatre Corp.,* 194 F. 846, 859 (1952).

of these guidelines and their historical application led one commentator to conclude that "in using these guides, courts have traveled many confusing and conflicting paths."[31]

However, the actual fees received by successful plaintiff lawyers bear little relationship to the court-awarded amount. The sum of money determined by the court is awarded to the plaintiff, not to his counsel. In most treble damage actions, the plaintiff's attorney works on a contingency fee basis; that is, his payment will constitute a percentage of the settlement or judgment (should there be one).[32] The percentage share will be negotiated prior to the action, and the counsel may negotiate to receive a retainer and some portion of the court-awarded attorney's fees as well. But the primary monetary inducement and reward for the plaintiff's attorney is the agreed upon percentage of the recovery.[33] That means the attorney may get nothing if the action is completely unsuccessful and is likely to receive much more than the court-determined fee if the suit is successful.

The payment of legal fees as a percentage of recovery has a colorful

31. Kelly, "Attorney's Fees," p. 1656. In the gypsum wallboard manufacturers conspiracy case, Judge Alfonso J. Zirpoli awarded 1.6 million dollars to two law firms who represented plaintiffs. This sizable sum was still less than the $3.3 million requested in what the judge saw as the "exaggerated and untenable" original claim. Judge Zirpoli stated that the fees should not be "niggardly" and "no more and no less" than deserved. "No more and no less" consisted of a base fee of $100 per hour for a partner's time, $50 per hour for associate counsel, and $15 per hour for a legal assistant. These amounts were then inflated by a weighted factor of 2.2, "because the hourly rate does not tell the full story." The law firm that originally initiated the action was assigned a weighted factor of 3 to make up for "substantial financial risk." "$9 Million Dollars Awarded in Legal Fees," *Washington Post,* August 25, 1974, p. 1A.

32. Joseph Alioto, "The Economics of a Treble Damage Case," *Antitrust Law Journal* 32 (1966): 87, 93; Kelly, "Attorney's Fees," p. 1673; Lee A. Freeman, "Attorney's Fees: A Search For A Rule Of Reason," *Antitrust Law Journal* 38 (1969): 721, 722–723.

33. While the contingency fee is the common payment mechanism in class action suits, the court retains jurisdiction over the percentage and amount of fees awarded in these suits. This is done partly to avoid the problems of some classes (or members) free riding on the efforts of those first assembling the class. See Kelly, "Attorney's Fees," pp. 1672–1678; Freeman, "Attorney's Fees," pp. 726–727.

history.[34] Prohibited by common law, Massachusetts still outlaws such arrangements, as do Canada, England, and most European countries. But the device is permissible in federal courts and in most state courts in this country. The central argument against such attorney-client financial arrangements is that they promote champerty and barratry; that is, the attorney has a financial incentive to promote or prolong a cause of action and to stir up legal strife through groundless and vexatious suits. In the United States, this apparent drawback has been considered outweighed by the benefits a contingent fee provided in helping persons afford legal services. There is little doubt that lawyers approve of the contingent fee payment mechanism:

> Indeed, a thorough search of the law reviews and related publications . . . has failed to produce a single article advocating abolition of the contingent fee contract.[35]

Our attention in treble damage suits is focused only on the plaintiff's legal fees, since the plaintiff is the originator of the action. Furthermore, our concern is with the size of these fees and the impact their size has upon the number of suits brought and the fervor with which they are fought. All three of these factors are affected by the widespread use of contingency fee arrangements by private parties in paying their counsel.

Data on total or average attorney's fees in litigated private suits and out-of-court settlements are unpublished, and the incomes of lawyers specializing in this practice are unavailable. Only a sketchy picture can be drawn about the size of these fees. Plaintiff's counsel generally receives 15 to 35 percent of the verdict and frequently also claims the full amount of the court-determined attorney's fees, should the case be fully litigated. Substantial fees thus accrue to some members of the antitrust bar, since most treble damage suits are settled out of court with pay-

---

34. John Y. Taggart, "Comment, Are Contingent Fees Ethical Where Client is Able to Pay a Retainer," *Ohio State Law Journal* 20 (Spring 1959): 329; Donald G. McNeil, "Some Historical Precedent for the Common Aversion to Paying Legal Fees," *The Brief Case* 9 (September 1959): 13; Jerry P. Rhodes, "Note, Acquiring Interest in Litigation—The Role of the Contingent Fee," *Kentucky Law Journal* 54 (Fall 1965): 155; Kenneth B. Hughes, "The Contingent Fee Contract in Massachusetts," *Boston University Law Review* 43 (Winter 1963): 1.

35. Hughes, "The Contingent Fee Contract," pp. 4–5.

ments running in the thousands and, in some cases, millions of dollars. For example, in the plumbing fixtures class action suits, the companies involved settled for the sum of $28 million. Of this, four private attorneys with specialities in treble damage actions shared an estimated $6 to $8 million.[36] Joseph Alioto received $2.3 million in fees for negotiating an out-of-court settlement of $16.2 million for the State of Washington and several of its municipalities in the aftermath of the electrical equipment conspiracy.[37] Alioto himself alluded to the changing fortunes of the plaintiff's counsel in describing the substantial settlements made after this notorious conspiracy case:

> A goodly part of this shifted silver wound up in the coffers of a new breed—a coterie of lawyers who up to that time had been prominently identified as antitrust defense lawyers.[38]

There is other evidence alluding to the sizable fees received by plaintiff's lawyers. Milton Handler claimed that, in class-action treble damage suits, "it is the attorneys, not the class members, who are true beneficiaries and the real parties in interest."[39] And at a meeting of the Antitrust Section of the American Bar Association, Victor Kramer warned darkly of a brewing "scandal in obtaining fees by plaintiff's lawyers in antitrust cases."[40] Certainly the antitrust literature contains adequate comment to suggest that treble damage suits represent a transfer of wealth from the corporate sector to the legal profession. Indeed such comments come unusually close to the meaning of Carl Sandburg's biting refrain:

> When the lawyers are through
> What is there left, Bob?

36. "Invisible Bilk: Price Fixers," *Washington Post,* June 6, 1971, p. A1.
37. Charles A. Bane, *The Electrical Equipment Conspiracies: The Treble Damage Actions* (New York: Federal Legal Publications, 1973), p. 257.
38. Alioto, "Economics of a Treble Damage Case," p. 88.
39. Milton Handler, "The Shift From Substantive to Procedural Innovation in Antitrust Suits: The Twenty-Third Annual Antitrust Review," *Columbia Law Review* 71 (January 1971): 1, 10.
40. Victor Kramer, "Current Antitrust Enforcement and Its Critics, Discussion," *Antitrust Law Journal* 40 (1971): 385.

Can a mouse nibble on it
And find enough to fasten a tooth in?[41]

If the returns from such legal endeavors are so high, what factor enable this labor market to behave like the soft drink and cigarett industries, that is, why, in response to these "high profits," is there no "new entry" that would bid down the high fees to a level commensurate with other legal work, adjusting for the risk factor.

Three hypotheses suggest themselves. First, the market for legal services may itself contain monopolistic elements.[42] Minimum fee schedules, ethical sanctions against price competition (referred to as chiseling), the difficulty the client has in evaluating the quality of the service (both ex ante and ex post), and other institutional restraints may prevent the fee structure from being diminished by competition. Second the fee structure may yet be bid down, but the process may take a long time to work itself out. Third, there remains the possibility, although it is exceedingly difficult to test, that the fees include substantial economic rent; that is, a payment that is higher than is necessary to elicit the services but that is paid because of genuine scarcity of the expertise needed to litigate such cases.

The second and third factors to be considered regarding contingence fees in private antitrust actions is their effect on the number of suits brought and the fervor with which they will be fought. The size of the fees affects the number of suits brought in two related ways. First, due to the fact that the fees appear to be substantial, there is an incentive for more lawyers to engage in and subtly to suggest and solicit such suits The current professional sanctions against bounty hunting inhibit this activity, but the larger the rewards, the less effective the inhibition.[43]

41. Carl Sandburg, "The Lawyers Know Too Much," cited in Martin Mayer *The Lawyers* (New York: Harper & Row, 1967), pp. 7–8; Richard Haas, "Professional and Ethical Aspects of Antitrust Class Actions," *Antitrust Law Journal* 41 (1972): 280; Marcus Mattson, "Private Treble Damage Actions: The Defendant's Side," *Antitrust Law Journal* 41 (1972): 551, 553.

42. Richard J. Arnould, "Pricing Professional Services: A Case Study of the Legal Service Industry," *Southern Economic Journal* 38 (April 1972): 495; "Note A Critical Analysis of Bar Association Minimum Fee Schedules," *Harvard Law Review* 85 (March 1972): 971, esp. pp. 976–982.

43. See the remarks of Judge John P. Fullam, "The Judicial View," *Antitrust Law Journal* 37 (1969): 866, 869–870. Also Simon N. Whitney, *Antitrust Policies* (New York: Twentieth Century Fund, 1958), 2:181.

Second, the manner in which the large fees are dispensed (i.e., the contingency system) means that there will be more treble damage suits brought because clients who are impecunious or risk averse or both will be more likely to file suit under this payments mechanism.

No definite assessment can be made with regard to the third factor. A traditional objection to contingent fees has been that the lawyer has an inducement to fight the suit beyond the bounds of justice in order to collect the incremental fees gained by the additional effort. In private antitrust damage suits, however, the charge has been made that the incentive is in the opposite direction. The potential percentage take is so high that, from the lawyer's standpoint, the point of diminishing returns from litigation is readily reached, causing the lawyer to negotiate a settlement for much less than his clients could obtain with additional litigation or bargaining. As Schwartz and Mitchell have shown, the economics of contingency bargaining is indeterminate, and, under different assumptions and conditions, can result in "too much" or "too little" effort by attorneys.[44] In any event there is evidence that within the antitrust bar the treble damage provision has come to represent a source of considerable income, because the bar has been able to capture for itself a significant portion of the judgments and settlements made under the aegis of section 4.

44. Murray L. Schwartz and Daniel J. B. Mitchell, "An Economic Analysis of the Contingent Fee in Personal-Injury Litigation," *Stanford Law Review* 22 (June 1970): 1125.

PART II: THE ANALYSIS

5

THE UNEASY CASE FOR
TREBLE DAMAGES

The Reciprocal Nature of Monopoly Damages

Chapter 1 demonstrated the public goods nature of antitrust. The mere proof of the existence of a public good does not by itself constitute an argument that the good should be provided by the government,[1] but is merely a demonstration that there is a potential for gains in consumer welfare and a suggestion that institutional arrangements to internalize the externalities be considered. The antitrust laws represent such a consideration, an attempt to provoke competitive behavior through a blending of public and private enforcement. But how efficient is this approach to the solution of the monopoly problem? This chapter evaluates the efficiency of the private ingredient of our antitrust policy mix (treble damage suits) while in chapters 6 and 7 the efficiency of the alternative of placing major reliance on public enforcement will be examined.

In discussing the merits of private antitrust enforcement, the concepts of liability and negligence, which have recently received attention in the literature of economics and law, have particular relevance.[2] In fact, the same conceptual questions that arise in regard to products liability and torts are present in the area of antitrust. In products liability, for ex-

1. James M. Buchanan, *The Demand and Supply of Public Goods* (Chicago: Rand McNally, 1968), Chap. 9. See also Roland N. McKean, "Government and the Consumer," *Southern Economic Journal* 39 (April 1973): 481.
2. Roland N. McKean, "Products Liability: Trends ond Implications," *University of Chicago Law Review* 38 (Fall 1970): 3; Richard A. Posner, "A Theory of Negligence," *Journal of Legal Studies* 1 (January 1972): 29; Richard A. Posner, "Strict Liability: A Comment," *Journal of Legal Studies* 2 (January 1973): 205.

ample, the efficiency issue is one of determining which party has the comparative advantage in avoiding the dangers of an exploding bottle, a defective tricycle, or whatever. The analogy in antitrust would be to the determination of the party to which the liability or tort for monopolizing should be assigned. And how strict (or conditional) should this rule be? Of course, present antitrust law places the liability on the monopolist; that is, the monopolist bears the penalty for anticompetitive behavior in the same sense that in the arena of products liability, firms are increasingly held liable for defective or negligently used products. But this rule is not conceptually inviolate nor historically *de rigueur,* as the law on products liability indicates.

In what has become one of the most widely cited contributions to the literature of economics and law, Ronald Coase demonstrated that the assignment of rules of liability does not affect private marginal costs of production, either in the short or long run, and therefore has no effect on the final composition of output.[3] This remarkable result assumes, as Coase noted, a costless market, or a world of no transactions, information, or monitoring costs. In this world, the laissez-faire policy solution of classical economics is the correct one in terms of maximizing the value of the economy's total output. To prove this proposition Coase assumed there were no incentives for people to attempt to free ride. In such a world, the assignment of "fault" for monopolistic distortions would also be irrelevant from an efficiency standpoint. The key proposition is this: if the fault or liability for damages resulting from overcharges were placed on the monopolist, he would cease monopolizing. If the fault were assigned to consumers, the end result would also be the elimination of monopoly as consumers smoothly and costlessly seek out monopolists and bribe them to behave competitively.

But it is the real world that concerns us. And Coase's analysis should provide a guide to the correct approach there as well, since Coase devoted the bulk of his attention to cases where bargaining and negotia-

3. R. H. Coase, "The Problem of Social Cost," *Journal of Law & Economics* 3 (October 1960): 1, as reprinted in William Breit and Harold M. Hochman, *Readings in Microeconomics,* 2d ed. rev. (New York: Holt, Rinehart, and Winston, 1971), at p. 484.

tion use up both time and resources.[4] Indeed, he stressed that in a world where the costs of market transactions are positive, there is no single policy or set of policies that would *a priori* lead to an efficient output. Public policy should attempt to balance the loss in the value of production against the gain in the value of production resulting from the policy.[5]

Put into the framework of the Coasian analysis, the costs involved in monopolistic behavior can be seen to have the same reciprocal nature as any externality. If liability is imposed on the consumer, a monopolist causes damage to the consumer of his product in the form of consumer's surplus lost. But if the liability is imposed on the monopolist through some form of antitrust law, the customer of the monopolist, in insisting through the law that the monopolistic behavior end, imposes a cost on the monopolist, the cost of lost monopoly returns. The question of "fault" is largely irrelevant in such a setting. The real issue is: what party to the transaction is the most efficient in preventing the misallocation resulting from monopoly?[6]

The alternatives are placing the liability entirely upon the monopolist (as prevailing antitrust laws do), placing the liability entirely upon the consumer, or placing the liability upon both. The present private action

---

4. In fact, the important contribution of Coase lies in this area. It is unfortunate that his central proposition—often referred to as "the Coase theorem"—has come to be identified with the world of costless transactions.

5. "The question is commonly thought of as one in which A inflicts harm on B and what has to be decided is: how should we restrain A? But this is wrong. We are dealing with a problem of a reciprocal nature. To avoid the harm to B would inflict harm on A. The real question to be decided is: should A be allowed to harm B or should B be allowed to harm A? The problem is to avoid the more serious harm. ... What answer should be given is, of course, not clear unless we know the value of what is obtained as well as the value of what is sacrificed to obtain it" Coase, "The Problem of Social Cost," p. 485.

6. The reciprocal nature of externalities was noted by Golda Meir, who taught the lesson to the Israeli Knesset. In the face of a rising rate of rapes, the politicians proposed a bill to protect the nation's women by placing them under curfew. Mrs. Meir pointed out that such a law would be punishing the victim, not the criminal, and suggested the curfew be placed on men. Both missed Coase's point. The Coase proposition is that if a curfew is to be imposed, it should be placed on that group whose loss would cause the least sacrifice of total output. Mrs. Meir's arguments before the Knesset were reported by Colman McCarthy in the *Washington Post,* August 8, 1973, p. A18.

system is one of strict liability, because the monopolistic seller must pay compensation. There are three major sources of inefficiency resulting from a private sector approach to eliminating anticompetitive behavior. The first we shall call the *perverse incentives effect;* the second, the *misinformation effect;* and the third, *reparations costs.*

The Efficiency of Private Actions

The Perverse Incentives Effect

By "perverse incentives effect" we mean that a private party neglects to modify his behavior when the damage done to him by the monopolistic firm exceeds the cost to him of avoiding that damage or that the consumer modifies his behavior in order to increase the damage done to him by the anticompetitive activity. Unless a consumer bears the cost of purchasing from a firm with market power, for instance, he has less motive to be a careful shopper and seek out competitive substitutes. In other words, the incentive to minimize his damages is weakened or disappears. He will not attempt to alter his customary purchasing practices to avoid being overcharged because he believes reparations will be forthcoming should he be found dealing with an antitrust violator. Moreover, the possibility of receiving more than the actual amount of damages magnifies the perverse incentives effect, since an individual has an incentive not only to neglect seeking out substitutes or finding ways of avoiding damages, but also even to suffer damages in order to benefit from the collection of threefold the amount of damages actually sustained. This incentive would exist whenever the expected value of the reparations is greater than the amount of the damage.

In a system where the probability of a conviction is high, the present trebling provision could put the expected value above the actual damage borne. As already noted, the fact that the probability is sufficiently high has led a number of authorities to recommend double damages as being more appropriate than treble damages for achieving the aims of antitrust policy. The Report of the Attorney General's National Committee to Study the Antitrust Laws noted:

> The inducement of mandatory trebled damages is no longer necessary to encourage suits by injured persons. The development of

both the procedural and substantive law, largely favorable to the plaintiff, plus the award of the attorney fees affords sufficient incentive to private antitrust actions.[7]

f this is the case, then the perverse incentives effect would be expected.

Some courts have recognized the inefficiencies that arise from the perverse incentives effect. Perhaps it will prove instructive to review ome of these cases, because they represent evidence that this effect exists under the present strict liability approach to antitrust law.

Sun Cosmetic Shoppe, a New York City retailer of perfumes and cosmetics, brought suit for treble damages against one of its suppliers, which, it claimed, had violated the Robinson-Patman Act.[8] The supplier, Elizabeth Arden Sales Corporation, furnished "demonstrators" to ome of its retail outlets to assist in the promotion of its cosmetics and toilet preparations. Sun Cosmetic Shoppe, however, was not provided with such a special sales clerk. The retailer claimed damages of $15,600 as a result of this "discrimination." The use of demonstrators by rival retail stores allegedly diverted this amount in profits from Sun to the favored stores.

With regard to the damages claimed, Judge Learned Hand, speaking for the court of appeals, stated that, if the loss caused by the diversion of Sun's customers to those retail outlets where the defendant furnished a demonstrator was greater than the cost of employing a demonstrator, Sun had an obligation to minimize its losses by employing one. Such a decision, making use of the concept of avoidable loss, introduced the element of negligent liability into what is normally a strict liability atmosphere. In so doing, Judge Hand recognized the equivalent of the perverse incentives aspect of private antitrust policy. Judge Hand's logical diagnosis, appealing as it might be to economists, has not persuaded his fellow jurists. For example, in *State Wholesale Grocers* v. *Great Atlantic & Pacific Tea Co.,* the court said:

> Judge Hand opined that if the loss caused by the diversion of
> business was greater than the cost of employing a demonstrator,

7. U.S., Justice Department, *Report of the Attorney General's National Committee to Study the Antitrust Laws,* 1955, p. 379.

8. *Sun Cosmetic Shoppe* v. *Elizabeth Arden Sales Corp.,* 178 F. 2d 150 (2d Cir. 1949).

the non-favored customer would have the duty to minimize the damages by employing one. This contention I am unable to accept . . . and I believe not in accordance not only with prevailing authority but the realities of economic facts of life as well.[9]

The latter view has prevailed, and the claim of perverse incentives is no currently a defense to antitrust prosecution.

The magnified perverse incentives effect was recognized by the cour in *American Can Co.* v. *Russellville Canning Co.*[10] In this case the operator of a green bean, spinach, turnip green, and mustard green canning company in Russellville, Arkansas, purchased its cans from the defendant. It claimed the defendant discriminated against it in price by giving quantity discounts to larger customers; by adopting a freight equalization plan with Fort Smith, Arkansas as a base; and by granting a discount to a canner adjacent to the defendant's can factory.

The trial produced a voluminous record, enormous detail about the canning industry, a prolonged legal contest involving two of the nation's most prominent law firms, and an important legal precedent. Of particular interest here is the refusal of the plaintiff to accept delivery of cans at the alleged discriminatory prices, an action that was then rewarded by a settlement of $375,000 in damages for losses incurred partly because the canning company had no cans. As Arvel Blaylock, the owner of the firm, put the matter in a telegram to American Can:

We could have been running turnip and mustard greens for the last ten or twelve days but you have failed to furnish and ship cans. . . . We are instructing our attorney to sue for damages for this loss.[11]

But the plaintiff could have received the cans had he been willing to pay the freight equalization for the eighty-mile journey from Fort Smith to Russellville.[12] The appellate court's statement in reversing the trial

9. 202 F. Supp. 768, 777 (N.D. Ill. 1961).
10. 191 F. 2d 38 (8th Cir. 1951).
11. Ibid., p. 47.
12. In 1945, this freight increment for all can shipments to Blaylock was less than $5,500. See *Russellville Canning Co.* v. *American Can Co.,* 87 F. Supp. 484, 492 (W.D. Ark. 1949).

court's judgment for the plaintiff is revealing of the kind of perverse incentives that can arise in a system of compensatory damages:

> Arvel Blaylock's conduct in dealing with these shipments and making claims for loss of profits was obviously strategic, and stemmed from the defendant's refusal to accede to his demand that cans be shipped to the plaintiff free of freight, as well as from his interest in enhancing his alleged damages for the purpose of this lawsuit.[13]

In the case of the electrical equipment conspiracy, there was evidence that the customers of this cartel were either aware (or had strong suspicions) that they were purchasing under a regime of rigged bidding. During the treble damage actions, a number of the interrogatories from the defendant companies sought to learn if their customers knew of the conspiracy prior to the government's successful prosecution and to what extent their customers had taken action, either by discussing the problem among themselves, seeking antitrust advice, or trying to shop with nonmember suppliers.[14] Charles Bane, in his detailed account of the treble damage actions against the cartel, indicates the tenuous nature of this defense for the electrical equipment companies. It would take substantial chutzpah to argue to a jury that the cartel's customers knew of the price rigging, when the top executives of the companies themselves fervently denied any knowledge of the activity.[15] Questions of legal strategy aside, in 1957 the managements of thirty-four utilities responded to a questionnaire and overwhelmingly indicated a belief that the electrical equipment manufacturers were conspiring on price and that the manufacturer's trade association was a vehicle for the fixing of prices and the allocation of markets.[16] The following deposition, taken from an employee of one of the damage seekers, is revealing:

A. There was certainly the feeling that our people shared with

---

13. 191 F. 2d 38, 55 (8th Cir. 1951).

14. Charles A. Bane, *The Electrical Equipment Conspiracies: The Treble Damage Actions* (New York: Federal Legal Publications, 1973), p. 202.

15. Ibid., p. 236.

16. Ibid., pp. 275, 290. This 1957 questionnaire, known as the Hogg questionnaire, was circulated by J. Donald Hogg, an executive with the Cleveland Electric Illuminating Company. The first indictments in this case came in February 1960.

many others that there was an artificial level being maintained
by the manufacturers.

Q. Now, when you say "artificial level" would you, again, be more
concrete?

A. I mean by getting together, . . .

Q. You say that was shared by many others?

A. Yes.

. . . It was shared by so many among the better utilities that it
was almost universally felt, I would say.[17]

In the defendant companies' national discovery program, a significant
memorandum of October 1954 was uncovered. It reported that at a
meeting of the Edison Electric Institute Committee on Purchasing and
Stores the answer was "unanimously given as 'yes' " to the question of
whether the "electrical manufacturers engage in the collusive setting of
prices, terms and conditions."[18]

Both economic theory and the empirical evidence, then, indicate that
the perverse incentives effect has militated against prudent conduct on
the part of customers, conduct that would have penalized firms with
market power. It also affords inducements to customers to behave perversely in hopes of collecting greater damages. One reason this behavior
receives little attention in antitrust case law is because it is viewed differently in antitrust than in the law of torts.[19]

In the law of torts, the doctrine of contributory fault or negligence
may enable a defendant to escape payment of damages, as does the
doctrine of *in pari delicto*. If the defendant can show that the plaintiff
himself was involved in wrongdoing or was negligent in his behavior, the
plaintiff may be precluded from securing damages. In antitrust the rule
regarding the plaintiff's behavior is precise: plaintiff's behavior is seldom, if ever, a bar to collection. As a result, the perverse incentives

17. Ibid., p. 289–290.
18. Ibid., p. 291.
19. This dichotomy is presented clearly and thoroughly in "Memorandum re
The Effects of Plaintiffs' Behavior," prepared in March 1964 for the General
Electric Company by the Denver law firm of Holme, Roberts, and Owen, as part
of its defense of treble damage claims. This document (hereafter cited as Memorandum) is in our files at the University of Virginia.

effect is given full sway.[20] Since 1951 the *American Can* decision has been eroded, for the courts now place far more emphasis on penalizing the antitrust violators, regardless of the "morals" of the plaintiff. As one court stated:

> ... Whatever equities may be present as between private litigants, they must yield to the overall public policy of the antitrust laws to prevent monopolies and restraint of trade.[21]

There have been some aberrations in this trend, but the Court's decision in *Perma Life Mufflers* v. *International Parts Corp.* seems to have settled the issue. Justice Black wrote that, though the plaintiff

> may be no less morally reprehensible than the defendant, ... the doctrine of in pari delicto, with its complex scope, contents, and effects, is not to be recognized as a defense to an antitrust action.[22]

Given this state of the law, many businessmen and consumers, cognizant of the potential for collecting damages, can view the antitrust laws as a type of insurance policy against "poor purchasing" and will at the margin reduce their precautionary purchasing efforts. The situation is analogous to that found in the field of insurance. Private insurance companies do not provide protection against fire or theft above the amount of actual loss because of what is known as "moral hazard." To overinsure would affect incentives and result in more carelessness, perhaps even in arson and other unlawful capers.

Obviously, not all businessmen or consumers are insensitive to the need for careful shopping and prudent purchasing nor do they all actively seek out monopoly prices in the expectation of being trebly rec-

---

20. In the past the doctrines of *in pari delicto* and "clean hands" were recognized as possible bars to a plaintiff's recovery and in some instances had been used successfully by defendants. According to these doctrines, plaintiff's own guilt or willful participation in the antitrust violation would represent a bar to recovery. Cf. *Bluefields S.S. Co.* v. *United Fruit Co.*, 243 F. 1 (3rd Cir. 1917); and *Eastman Kodak* v. *Blackmore*, 277 F. 694 (2d Cir. 1921). But see *Kiefer-Stewart Co.* v. *Joseph E. Seagram & Sons*, 340 U.S. 211 (1951); and Memorandum, at pp. 15–32.

21. *Trebuhs Realty Co.* v. *News Syndicate Co.*, 107 F. Supp. 595, 599 (S.D.N.Y. 1952).

22. 392 U.S. 134, 139–40 (1968).

ompensed at a later date. Some are possibly unaware of the reparation feature of the antitrust laws or could not, without exerting enormous efforts, learn that they are buying from a cartel or that they have been damaged by an anticompetitive merger. At the margin, however, some will exhibit the perverse incentives effect by not protecting against easily avoidable damages or by actively seeking to increase the damage done to them by alleged antitrust violators. Economic theory predicts that the greater the probability of collecting damages, and the greater the damage awards allowed by law, the greater will this incentive be operative.[23]

The Misinformation Effect

By "misinformation effect" we mean the propensity for a private party to claim that anticompetitive behavior has taken place when it has not. In other words, the misinformation effect appears when allegations are generated about violations of the antitrust laws that are not grounded in fact. Note that the distinction between this effect and the perverse incentives effect is that in the latter case the individual actually sustains damages. In the misinformation effect, there is no damage done to the plaintiff, only an allegation of damages. This type of suit is commonly referred to as a "nuisance suit," and it is brought in the hopes that defendants will pay some amount of money rather than go to trial. As a consequence of such suits, prices are higher, because this litigation, by raising costs, has the same effect as a tax levied by plaintiffs on defendants.

---

23. Richard A. Posner has suggested to us that under certain conditions the perverse incentives effect might not result in serious misallocative problems. After all, if this effect involves a willingness to increase purchases from a monopolist, buying more than would otherwise be the case at the monopoly price, the deadweight loss is reduced. However, further reflection shows that this mitigating influence is unlikely. If the compensation payments to the consumer must come from the monopolist, these payments are equivalent to a tax on the producer-monopolist. The more he sells to the consumer who is recompensed, the greater the tax. Hence his costs rise, which causes him to produce less, thus *increasing* deadweight loss. It is not clear on which side of the ledger the balance of the effects would fall. Moreover, the belief that the perverse incentives effect might reduce deadweight loss is a second-best argument. It says that the distortions caused by monopoly can be offset by distortions caused by the perverse incentives effect. Once second-best considerations are introduced, the welfare implications of any policy are difficult to discern.

Nuisance suits are quite common in personal injury cases.[24] And the present structure of private treble damage suits, with their emphasis on strict liability, offers even greater incentives for suits of this nature. Given the attitudes of the managers of large corporations toward risk, lawyers and their clients may see businessmen as tantalizingly vulnerable. As we argue later in more detail, the directors of large enterprises typically prefer a completely certain but relatively small loss to the unpredictable payment of a relatively large (even if improbable) loss. In such circumstances, an out-of-court settlement with claimants who have brought groundless charges appears to be the prudent course of conduct.

This is particularly true of antitrust violations where the outcome of a suit is unpredictable. For a nuisance suit to pose a credible threat to a defendant, there must be difficulty in predicting the outcome of the suit. If it were against the law to be over six feet tall and there were a bounty for detecting the guilty, short people would not be likely candidates for nuisance suits. The precise nature of the offense would enable them confidently and inexpensively to go to trial and prove their innocence.

Such a situation does not exist with regard to the antitrust laws. Certain offenses, to be sure, can be readily litigated in a predictable fashion: for example, the per se rule against price fixing is well established. But in other areas of the law, where private antitrust actions are common, the precise nature of the activity that might be found unlawful is less clear. For example, a seller sued for damages stemming from an alleged violation of the Robinson-Patman Act (a statute that even the Supreme Court admits is not known for its precision) cannot accurately predict, from the facts, eventual guilt or innocence. Refusals to sell, franchise terminations, exclusive dealer arrangements, territorial agreements, and other such "marketing violations," as well as nonhorizontal mergers, involve so many combinations and permutations of fact situations that a confident prediction of guilt or innocence is difficult.

A second problem that makes antitrust litigation more unpredictable than other kinds of suits is the question of who has standing to sue. If only certain well-defined groups are allowed to bring suits, then de-

24. H. Lawrence Ross, *Settled Out of Court: The Social Process of Insurance Claims Adjustments* (Chicago: Aldine Publishing Company, 1970), pp. 204–211.

fendants sued by ineligible parties need not seriously consider out-of court settlement proposals by the plaintiff. But the ambiguous issue of who has legal standing to bring suits compounds the prediction difficulty for defendants in private antitrust actions. The ingenious application by some plaintiffs of such novel doctrines as *parens partriae* and *cy pres* illustrate the innovative ideas used in seeking standing to sue.[25] While these particular attempts may not receive judicial favor, the decision in *Hanover* stands as evidence that courts can radically alter the conventional wisdom on which groups can be found to have standing.[26] Until the concept of standing can take on precise analytical content, thus allowing defendants to make confident predictions about who can sue them, plaintiffs will have further reason and enhanced ability to exploit the misinformation effect.

Even if the determination of guilt or innocence could be clearly specified, the present law on private damage suits offers significant incentives for a risk averse management to settle spurious claims out of court because of the difficult task of estimating the size of the judgment. The economic incentive for a plaintiff to generate misinformation regarding

25. The *cy pres* doctrine is the doctrine that enables courts to distribute charitable bequests that literally cannot be fulfilled. See "Charities," *American Jurisprudence*, 2d ed. (1964), vol. 15. As applied to private damage suits, the *cy pres* doctrine would mean that even if conditions make it impossible to directly compensate injured persons, plaintiffs should be able to sue for damages and award the reparations in some general next-best fashion. The doctrine is advocated by "Comment, Damage Distribution in Class Actions: The *Cy Pres* Remedy, *University of Chicago Law Review* 39 (Winter 1972): 448. The doctrine of *parens patria* permits individual states, as quasi-sovereigns, to protect their interests—historically with regard to disputes with other states over such matters as interstate embargoes, waterways, or externality problems. In the context of antitrust enforcement, the doctrine would permit a state to sue for damages not only with regard to its own purchases but also as representing a class of its citizens who had been directly injured by the antitrust violation. It could even represent all of the citizens of the state if the antitrust violation can be shown to have adversely affected the state's overall economy and prosperity, but this usage has not fared well in the courts. See *Hawaii* v. *Standard Oil Co. of California,* 405 U.S. 25 (1972). For support of this doctrine, see Morris D. Forkosch, *Antitrust and the Consumer* (Buffalo: Dennis Publishing Co., 1956), pp. 311–344; and "Comment Wrongs Without Remedy: The Concept of *Parens Patriae* Suits for Treble Damages Under the Antitrust Laws," *Southern California Law Review* 43 (1970): 570.

26. *Hanover Shoe, Inc.* v. *United Shoe Machinery Corp.*, 245 F. Supp. 258 (M.D. Pa. 1965); 377 F. 2d 776 (3rd Cir. 1967); 392 U.S. 481 (1968).

the extent of damages is obvious. For every extra dollar of damages claimed, there is the prospect of gaining three. The prospect is not a will-o'-the-wisp. Current case laws clearly states that a successful plaintiff is not to be deprived of damages simply because the amount of the damages cannot be precisely measured. As the Supreme Court indicated:

> the constant tendency of the courts is to find *some way* in which damages can be awarded where a wrong has been done. Difficulty of ascertainment is no longer confused with right of recovery "for a proven invasion of the plaintiff's rights."[27]

Judge Herbert Goodrich's statement in *Momand* v. *Universal Film Exchange* is also illustrative:

> The law has gone far to ease that burden [of strict requirements of proof as to exact quantity of damage] by permitting proof of losses *which border on the speculative,* in order to implement the policy of the antitrust laws.[28]

In personal injury cases, the distinction between proof of injury and proof of damages usually can be drawn with clarity; in antitrust the task of conceptually distinguishing the proof of fact of damage and the proof of the amount of damages is much less clear. Nevertheless, in private antitrust cases, as mentioned earlier, though courts purportedly require plaintiffs to prove rigorously that they have been *damaged,* "exactness and precision" are not then required in proving the *amount* of the damage. Given the capricious nature of the calculation of damages caused by anticompetitive activity, the plaintiff's possession of enormous leeway in offering these calculations means that defendants must give credence to almost any private suit.

The likelihood that misinformation will be generated is further heightened by the presence of juries in many private antitrust suits. This means a defendant company, usually a larger firm than the plaintiff, will face the prospect of litigating complicated economic issues before what Herbert Spencer called "a group of twelve people of average ignorance."

27. *Bigelow* v. *RKO Radio Pictures, Inc.,* 327 U.S. 251, 265–66 (1946), emphasis added.
28. 172 F. 2d 37, 43 (1st Cir. 1948), emphasis added.

Applying the ambiguous legal principles to the facts of the case can encourage portrayal of the issue in moral or emotional terms. As one antitrust lawyer expressed the matter:

> In triple damage antitrust actions . . . the jury, and for that matter the court, reaches its verdict or finding motivated by emotional factors and rational factors are used only to justify the verdict or finding after it has been arrived at emotionally.[29]

In another context, a plaintiff's lawyer remarked:

> The plaintiff wins because the jury determines that the plaintiff has been wronged or, in the language of the streets, has been kicked around by the defendants and is thus entitled to some recompense.[30]

Difficulties in predicting the outcome of litigation, the almost whimsical standards of damage estimation, the uncertainties of a jury trial concerned with complicated legal and economic issues—any of these could generate the misinformation manifested in nuisance suits. The coalescense of all of these factors in private antitrust enforcement makes nuisance suits more likely in this area of law than in many others.

Documenting the misinformation effect is difficult. Cases settled out of court do not enter the public record, and parties on both sides have an incentive to dissemble the complete circumstances behind their decisions to settle. The defendants would not be anxious to divulge the amount they have paid out in what they may recognize is a groundless claim lest they invite stockholder reprisals or similar suits from other plaintiffs. Plaintiffs, in turn, are not anxious to reveal their winnings because they are behaving strategically. Such disclosures might affect their ability to make such claims in the future.

The upshot is that, however groundless a claim might be in reality, every defendant must attach some positive probability to the prospect of losing if the claim is litigated. In such cases, a nuisance suit can

29. Thomas M. Scanlon, "The Jury's Viewpoint," *Antitrust Law Journal* 38 (1969): 76.
30. Maxwell M. Blecher, "Discussion," *Antitrust Law Journal* 38 (1969): 50, 52.

become a realistic threat if the defendant fails to settle on terms agreed to by the plaintiff. In fact, the term nuisance suit may be inappropriate. The amount of damages claimed, particularly under the umbrella of a class action, can be substantial. A rational management, faced with the vagaries just mentioned, may settle out of court—not so much to eliminate a nuisance—but as an *in terrorem* response to the repercussions of an (even slim) chance of losing.[31]

Reparations Costs

There is a third inefficiency associated with the treble damage provision of the antitrust laws. Private enforcement presently involves the use of resources in the determination and allocation of the damages themselves, contrasted to public enforcement where no reparations are made. The compensation element of private enforcement further complicates and extends the usage of multidistrict litigation, out-of-court negotiations, legal strategy, and all of the other trappings of reparations-induced private damage actions. The complications of these suits, particularly in the form of class actions, has already engendered much critical comment and increased the congestion in the federal courts.

---

31. That this possibility might pose a serious problem apparently has been noted only once in Congress. During debates on the treble damage provision of the Clayton Act the lone voice objecting to section 4, clearly on the grounds of its potential "misinformation effect" was that of Congressman Jefferson Levy of New York. In response to the argument of Congressman Edwin Webb of North Carolina that the private actions provision would provide incentives for widespread enforcement and thereby serve as a powerful deterrent, Levy asked: "Does the bill provide any means by which the business interests of the country can be protected? Suppose a lot of blackmailers bring suit for damages against businessmen all over the United States. Is there any protection provided for the business interests of the country?"

In his reply to this sensible inquiry, Webb skirted the issue: "Yes, there is protection for the businessman. Somebody may go down and undertake to squat on your magnificent estate in Virginia, but you can put him off. You cannot prevent him from squatting but you can bring a suit and put him off."

But Levy persisted: "But there is nothing to prevent businessmen from being blackmailed? This bill is all in favor of the complainants." U.S., *Congressional Record,* 63d Cong., 2d Sess., 1914, 51, Part 16, 16275, cited in U.S., Congress, House, Committee on the Judiciary, *Hearings, Discretionary Treble Damages in Private Antitrust Suits,* 83rd Cong., 1st Sess., 1954, p. 58. Congressman Levy's "magnificent estate" in Virginia was Thomas Jefferson's Monticello.

Moral Hazard Costs, Reparations Costs, and Deterrence

The preceding discussion showed that from an efficiency standpoint the present reliance upon reparations to private parties in antitrust enforcement has three defects. First, if expected payments to plaintiffs do not completely deter monopolistic activity, private actions are a fertile source of perverse incentives. Second, the use of reparations to stimulate private actions generates misinformation in the form of nuisance suits. Third, real resources are utilized not only in the conviction of violators but in the determination of damages. The latter defect involves the use of scarce resources that could be put to better uses. Unlike the first two defects of private actions, the costs involved are a direct effect of the treble damage provision and were clearly intended by the original proponents of the antitrust laws. Nevertheless, the proliferation of treble damage cases in the courts and the congestion problems accompanying it suggest that a search for less costly alternatives would be fruitful. Aside from incarceration (which is not a viable option given the inherent inability to identify individual violators) two alternatives remain: dissolution and fines. To these possibilities we now turn.

6

THE DISSOLUTION SOLUTION:
AN ILLUSION?

The Economics of Structural Relief

The alternative to private enforcement through the treble damage incentive is public enforcement, relying mainly upon structural relief, fines, and incarceration. Whether these instruments are viable alternatives depends upon the magnitude of their costs in relation to the benefits ultimately derived from their use. The jail penalty has an inherent defect, the inability precisely to identify the actual instigators of the antitrust violation, that makes judges and juries understandably reluctant to use this weapon. In the chapter that follows we shall show another disadvantage of the jail penalty: any level of deterrence it accomplishes can be secured at less cost through an appropriate fine. In this chapter we shall limit our discussion to the economics of structural relief and devote chapter 7 to financial penalties.

As with any other penalty, an economic analysis of structural relief is concerned with the welfare implications of its use. That is to say, do the costs of this instrument swamp any benefits that may accompany its application? The advocate of structural relief must believe that any economic benefits of DDD must come from either or both of the following sources: (1) the deterrent impact such a measure might have on those firms contemplating or now engaging in antitrust violations that would be subject to this penalty; (2) captured welfare triangles that might accrue from the actual remedying of monopolistic market structures in the industries where this instrument is applied.

The deterrent impact requires only brief comment. DDD is not recognized as a penalty but rather as a remedy under present antitrust law.

However, to the economist that is a distinction without a difference if the imposition of this measure inflicts costs upon the firm in excess of any compensation arising from the dismemberment. For then the remedy is the same as an economic penalty. After all, a firm would have no pref-erence if it had a choice between paying a $50,000 fine to the state as a *penalty* for an antitrust violation or incurring $50,000 in fees and costs to divest itself of an asset in complying with the *remedy* of structural relief. The efficacy of either the penalty of the fine or the so-called remedy of DDD depends on whether the cost incurred is greater than the expected benefits from violating the law. Just as in the case of fines and incarceration, the value of the dissolution penalty depends upon its deterrent effects in relation to the costs of utilizing it. From the economic perspective, structural relief thus can be seen as another penalty in the antitrust tool kit.

The legal view that structural relief is a remedy and not a penalty would be correct only if it were assumed that the firm incurred no costs in divesting itself of the assets and received full compensation. Of course, this assumption is unrealistic. Full compensation is unlikely, and the complexities of divestiture outlined in chapter 3 are suggestive of the legal fees, accounting difficulties, organizational and morale prob-lems, as well as the search costs that are part and parcel of compliance with a DDD directive. Such costs are no doubt sizable enough to provide a measure of deterrence; and these are real costs to society, not trans-fers.[1] It should be recognized, however, that any reduction in monopoly profits due to DDD, while a financial loss to the firm's owners, will not just be a deterrent to structural violations. For anything earned during the violation would be sunk. The old adage "bygones are forever by-gones" applies as much to sunk revenues as to sunk costs. A balance must be struck between these two effects before a judgment can be made as to whether structural relief is a remedy or a penalty.

1. Donald F. Turner, a one-time advocate of massive deconcentration and a former head of the Antitrust Division, now expresses concern about the substan-tial social costs that might accompany Government sponsored deconcentration proposals. Testifying on the Hart bill he said: "there would be extensive costs in embarking on such . . . a program. The costs of investigating and litigating such . . . imprecise issues . . . both for the Government and the private parties in-volved, would alone be substantial." See U.S., Senate, Committee on the Judi-ciary, Subcommittee on Antitrust and Monopoly, *Hearings, The Industrial Reorganization Act,* 93d Cong., 1st Sess., March and May, 1973, p. 276.

The second source of alleged benefits from structural relief comes from any captured welfare triangles that would accrue from altering market structures. The magnitude of these triangles in the United States economy has been the subject of much debate. Suffice it to say here that if, as has been argued,[2] the extent of welfare loss due to monopoly is de minimus, the economic case for DDD (at least on any significant scale) is scuttled. Similarly, structural relief would make no economic sense if an industry's structure were not, in some predictable fashion, related to that industry's performance. If monopoly welfare losses are small, or not related to market structure, the case for DDD can only be made on such noneconomic grounds as the virtue of attaining the Jeffersonian ideal of small independent proprietors.

Even assuming a significant welfare loss associated with market structure, two questions remain to be asked: (1) what happens to economies of scale under structural relief; and (2) what effect do the benchmarks commonly associated with DDD have on economic welfare? If significant scale economies are sacrificed through DDD or the use of the benchmarks suggested as triggers for DDD themselves entail substantial costs, then any benefits from structural relief might be vitiated. This issue will now be considered.

The Preservation of Economies of Scale

In his seminal article on dissolution, George E. Hale pointed out a potential conflict between structural reorganization and efficiency loss. He wrote: "In formulating a norm of size for business units the demands of a 'pure' competitive order must be balanced against the engineering requirements of efficient mass production."[3] But Hale provided no means of devising this norm. He only noted the absence of such formulations in the literature on business efficiency.

Much more recently Oliver Williamson provided the theoretical framework for viewing the potential trade-off of social losses resulting

2. Arnold C. Harberger, "Monopoly and Resource Allocation," *American Economic Review* (Proceedings) 44 (May 1954): 77–87. Cf. David R. Kamerschen, "An Estimation of the 'Welfare Losses' from Monopoly in the American Economy," *Western Economic Journal* 4 (Summer 1966): 221–237.

3. George E. Hale, "Trust Dissolution: Atomizing Business Units of Monopolistic Size," *Columbia Law Review* 40 (April 1940): 615, 631.

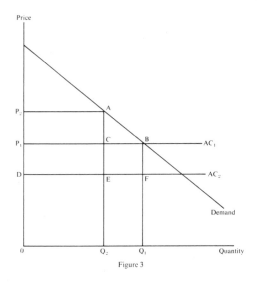

Figure 3

from monopoly and social benefits deriving from economies of scale.[4] Williamson's model was presented as a tool for developing an antimerger policy to deal with those mergers that might yield both market power and efficiencies in production. However, his model can also be used for studying a closely related and more important problem, that of dissolving a single firm that possesses market power, when the dissolution might remove the market power but would also destroy certain operating efficiencies. To put the matter tersely, in the case of mergers, what is the appropriate policy toward those mergers that will raise price but lower costs? Again, in the case of firms with market power, what is the appropriate policy regarding the use of structural relief that would lower price but also raise costs? Consider the two issues in turn.

Figure 3 depicts a proposed merger that will yield economies of scale and also give the resulting firm additional market power. The firm's premerger average cost function is the horizontal line AC_1. Assume that it sells its product at $P_1 = AC_1$ and produces at output Q_1, which is the competitive price and output. After making an acquisition, its costs of production are lowered to AC_2, and, because of increased market power, it maximizes profits at price P_2. Within the framework of this simple static model, society benefits from an economic standpoint if the gain in the value of resources saved, represented by the rectangle P_1CDE, is greater than the deadweight loss in consumer's surplus, shown by the triangle ABC. In its most pristine form, the Williamson trade-off model means that if area ABC exceeds P_1CDE, the merger should be stopped; if it is less than P_1CDE, the merger should be allowed, or at least viewed with more sympathy. Williamson develops some estimates of the relative trade-offs for three different price elasticities of demand. He shows that even with high elasticities of demand, a relatively small percentage reduction in average costs is adequate to offset relatively generous percentage increases in price. As he indicated:

> The naive model thus supports the following proposition: a merger which yields nontrivial real economies must produce substantial market power and result in relatively large price increases for the net allocative effects to be negative.[5]

But the Supreme Court has asserted that:

> surely one premise of an antimerger statute . . . is that corporate growth by internal expansion is socially preferable to growth by acquisition.[6]

The Court, perhaps unwittingly, put its finger on the most important technical caveat concerning the Williamson proposition as it relates to merger policy: most cost-saving advantages of combination are as likely to be available to the acquiring firm through internal expansion as through merger. However, internal expansion is not likely to have as adverse an effect upon competition as combination. Consequently, a hostile policy toward anticompetitive (albeit efficiency inducing) mergers,

---

5. Ibid. p. 23. Williamson stressed that this proposition is the preliminary conclusion from the model, and he presented a number of important qualifications and extensions in his paper. See also Williamson's "Economies as an Antitrust Defense: Correction and Reply," *American Economic Review* 58 (December 1968): 1372–1376.

6. *U.S.* v. *Philadelphia National Bank,* 374 U.S. 321 at 370 (1963).

with regard either to preventing them or dissolving them, is not likely (over time) to deprive society of the cost savings. In other words, society may be able to stop the merger and still capture the rectangle P_1CDE.

The most important empirical caveat with regard to the Williamson proposition as it relates to merger policy is that the economic evidence provides little grounds for the belief that mergers make a significant contribution to securing economies of scale.[7] That is, the literature indicates that mergers are not likely to foster a rectangle P_1CDE of substantial size.

The Williamson model is also useful in understanding the complex trade-offs in the case of monopoly (or shared monopoly). Here, presumably, the dominant firm's market share may have been achieved through internal growth, for example, the construction of lower cost plant(s), which gives it a cost function illustrated by AC_2 in figure 3. Assume that these costs are so low (or the economies of scale so great relative to the size of the market) as to provide the firm with the market power to charge price P_2. If dissolution were applied to the firm, an action that would reduce the market power but eliminate some of the economies of scale, the resultant trade-off can be shown by the diagram. Assume corporate surgery yielded new rivals and more vigorous price competition so that price dropped to P_1. Assume also that the loss in economies accruing from the DDD raised average costs to AC_1. The areas ABC (the social gain) and P_1CDE (the social loss) indicate the relevant magnitudes for weighing the DDD policy.

Three basic considerations are involved in the application of the trade-off model to single firms with monopoly power. The first harks

7. See the review of the literature by Jesse Markham, "Survey of the Evidence and Findings on Mergers," *Business Concentration and Price Policy,* Conference of the Universities–National Bureau for Economic Research (Princeton: Princeton University Press, 1955), pp. 154–167; also R. B. Heflebower, "Corporate Mergers: Policy and Economic Analysis," *Quarterly Journal of Economics* 77 (November 1963): 537–558; and George J. Stigler, "Monopoly and Oligopoly by Merger," *American Economic Review,* Proceedings 40 (May 1950): 23–34. If mergers were actually prompted by cost-cutting considerations, one might expect their frequency to vary inversely with the level of business activity. Although this expectation was believed by no less an economist than Karl Marx, it has not been fulfilled.

back to the point made with regard to antimerger enforcement. In the case of strict antimerger enforcement, it seemed likely that any efficiencies lost by barring or undoing a merger eventually would be recouped through internal growth. But if AC_2 is raised as a result of DDD applied to a single firm that had exploited economies of production or marketing, especially in a single plant, it is much less likely that the resultant higher costs will come down after the dismemberment. In the formulation of the problem in figure 3, by definition they would not do so. If AC_1 represents the lowest costs obtainable in the suboptimal operations instituted by the relief decree, then area P_1CDE has been lost to society.

The second consideration is that the cost curves neatly portrayed in figure 3 are not well defined in the case of firms with substantial market power. To be sure, an average cost curve that represents the lowest attainable costs at various levels of output exists on a conceptual level. But there is reason to believe that, for firms with market power (even those that are most facile in knowing or locating these cost minima), the minima nevertheless cannot be empirically ascertained for antitrust purposes. For example, the lowest cost curve may in fact be AC_2 for some dominant firm with market power. But for reasons stemming from its insulated market position, the tax laws, the separation of its management from the shareholders, or some combination of these (or other) factors, the firm may elect to operate on AC_1, perhaps taking some of its monopoly profits in the form of higher managerial salaries and perquisites or increased management laxity toward performing tasks.[8] This characteristic is what J. R. Hicks casually referred to as the best of all monopoly profits (the "quiet life") and is a phenomenon that has been much more carefully described by Leibenstein as involving X-Efficiency.[9] Further complicating the definition of the cost curve AC_2 is its propensity to be capitalized and therefore, in terms of its empirical identification, elevated. Milton Friedman has argued that it is the

8. Williamson found evidence that the reported profits of some oligopolistic firms were understated because they absorbed "some fraction of actual profits in executive salaries and possibly in perquisites of a variety of sorts." See his "Managerial Discretion and Business Behavior," *American Economic Review* 53 (December 1963): 1032–1055, at p. 1055.

9. H. Leibenstein, "Allocative Efficiency vs. 'X-Efficiency,'" *American Economic Review* 56 (June 1966): 392–415.

capitalization of monopoly returns into costs, both economic and ac-counting, that hinders the statistical measurement of cost curves.[10] This argument means that in practice the simple trade-off model becomes an empty box; it cannot be applied in concrete situations to examine or estimate the potential trade-offs involved.

The third consideration can be treated very briefly. The conventional wisdom in economics with regard to economies of scale is that for a broad cross-section of manufacturing industries the current levels of concentration will not be "dictated" by economies of scale.[11] On the contrary, small and medium-size plants often can produce at lower average costs than their larger counterparts. The evidence is even stronger that enormous corporate units need not be left intact in order for society to receive dynamic economies; that is, a supply of innovations in products and production techniques.[12] Many advocates of a DDD program, of course, base their arguments upon this evidence, contending that corporate surgery is unlikely to inflict diseconomies and is likely to promote innovation. This argument fails to take into account, however, that the mere survival or even the prosperity of a small firm in a highly concentrated industry cannot be taken as proof of that firm's efficiency. Its survival may be wholly due to its existence under the shelter of the price umbrella erected by the industry's oligopolists.

There remains the issue of whether one can move from an estimate of minimum optimum size for a firm to the prediction that any ongoing firm larger than this can be dissolved with no significant losses in effi-ciency. This prediction is premised on the notion that a firm is es-sentially a legal entity. One distinguished economist who held this view was Frank A. Fetter. He argued:

A combination of corporations is not a mess of scrambled eggs but

10. Milton Friedman, *Price Theory, A Provisional Text* (Chicago: Aldine Publishing Company, 1962), pp. 139–147.

11. The literature on this point is extensive. See John Blair, *Economic Concentration: Structure, Behavior and Public Policy* (New York: Harcourt, Brace, 1972), chaps. 5–8; F. M. Scherer, *Industrial Market Structure and Economic Performance* (Chicago: Rand McNally, 1970), pp. 72–103; Roger Sherman and Robert Tollison, "Public Policy Toward Oligopoly: Dissolution and Scale Economies," *Antitrust Law & Economics Review* 4 (Summer 1971): 77–90.

12. Blair, *Economic Concentration,* chaps. 9–10; Scherer, *Industrial Market Structure,* chap. 15.

a network of legal contracts. It is not a Gordian knot which cannot be untied. What the ingenuity of corporation lawyers has put together the ingenuity of other lawyers and the courts can take apart.[13]

According to this conception, if a minimum optimum size firm in some particular industry is one with 10 percent of a market, and firm X, a mere legal figment, has 20 percent of this market, firm X could be divided into two firms, each with 10 percent market shares, and no great problems would result. The dissolution experience under the 1935 Public Utility Holding Company Act is sometimes cited as evidence of the ease with which large firms can be dismembered.[14]

In economic orthodoxy, a firm is much more than a legal instrument. The firm is above all a product of economic forces. This view has its origins in Ronald Coase's seminal article on the nature of the firm.[15] To Coase, a firm arises because of the costs of using the price mechanism, especially the costs of learning about prices and the costs of making detailed contracts for each use of every one of a firm's inputs. Coase showed how the substitution of "central planning" by a firm could greatly reduce these costs. As he put it:

> It is true that contracts are not eliminated when there is a firm but they are greatly reduced. A factor of production (or the owner thereof) does not have to make a series of contracts with the factors with whom he is co-operating within the firm, as would be necessary, of course, if this cooperation were as a direct result of the working of the price mechanism. For this series of contracts is substituted one.[16]

The Coasian concept of the firm represents a major hurdle for ad-

13. Quoted in U.S., Congress, Temporary National Economic Committee, *Final Report and Recommendations,* 77th Cong., 1st Sess., 1941, p. 661.
14. Walter Adams, U.S., Congress, Senate, Committee on the Judiciary, Subcommittee on Antitrust and Monopoly, *Hearings, Economic Concentration,* part 1, 88th Cong., 2d session, 1964, pp. 250–251; Howard J. Trienens, "The Utility Act as a Solution to Sherman Act Problems," *Illinois Law Review* 44 (July-August 1949): 331–339.
15. R. H. Coase, "The Nature of the Firm," *Economica* 14 (n.s.) (November 1937): 386–405.
16. Ibid., p. 391.

herents of DDD. First, it suggests the possibility that a firm exists because, in its present form with its current resources, its size is the one at which it can organize production and exchange less expensively than through either the market mechanism or in the shape of some other firm size.[17] Second, Coasian firms, even within the same industry, will vary in size. Some entrepreneurs (or managers) will be less likely to make mistakes and can therefore efficiently organize a larger bundle of inputs (thus making for a larger firm) than other entrepreneurs.

In sum, no clear conclusions seem possible regarding the interface of DDD and the preservation of efficiency. The conceptual underpinnings of the economics involved can be articulated with a modicum of precision, but the application of this analysis to specific DDD problems would be extremely complicated.

The Benchmarks for Structural Relief

The literature concerning the appropriate means of identifying and selecting antitrust defendants is voluminous and the analyses it contains are by no means in harmony. Candidates for structural relief are generally to be selected on the basis of some combination of the following benchmarks:

a. the firm's market share
b. the joint market shares of the leading firms in an industry
c. the firm's profits
d. the firm's absolute size
e. the firm's (or industry leaders') price behavior

Specifically, a high market share, a highly concentrated industry, a substantial rate of return, immense sales or assets, or a pattern of rigid or harmonious prices are suggested signals for DDD proceedings.

Whether or not any or all of these are in fact indicators of monopoly power will not be discussed here. However, all of them, especially the

17. "[A] firm will tend to expand until the costs of organizing an extra transaction within the firm become equal to the costs of carrying out the same transaction by means of an exchange on the open market or the costs of organising in another firm" (Ibid., p. 395).

first four, have important efficiency implications for the adoption of any DDD program, implications that go beyond the conventional questions of whether these variables are indicative of anticompetitive behavior. The two crucial points are these: (1) Can these variables be measured or meaningfully estimated prior to dismemberment? (2) If these variables are allowed as a standard for instigating DDD proceedings, will their very acceptance have inefficiency implications? Consider first the problem of measurement.

Determining a firm's market share or an industry's degree of concentration is predicted upon the delineation of an economically meaningful "relevant market"; that is, including those products readily substitutable for one another and excluding all others. To disciples of Edward H. Chamberlin, such a delineation is impossible. According to their view, for different people under varying circumstances, widely diverse types of goods or services may be reasonable substitutes. However, most economists retain the concept of the industry or relevant market, and economic analysis provides the most useful device for trying to delineate meaningful markets: cross-elasticity of demand.

But cross-elasticity's use in the adversary contest of antitrust trials has not always been punctilious, and courts have not consistently been successful in their exegesis of the concept. For example, economists probably would agree that cross-elasticity was correctly defined and used in the *du Pont* decision—but only in the minority opinion.[18] Furthermore, in antimerger cases, where market delineation has become the first (and often the decisive) step in deciding the action, the courts seem to have given the government almost carte blanche in selecting a market formation most favorable to its case. The result has not always been one consistent with respectable economic analysis.[19]

In addition, the current availability of data would seriously hamper any widescale DDD efforts based on market shares. The Bureau of the Census provides the only source of concentration ratios consistently

18. *U.S. v. E. I. du Pont de Nemours,* 351 U.S. 377 (1956); George W. Stocking and Willard F. Mueller, "The Cellophane Case and the New Competition," *American Economic Review* 45 (March 1955): 27–63.
19. Kenneth G. Elzinga and Thomas F. Hogarty, "The Delineation of Geographic Markets in Antimerger Cases," *The Antitrust Bulletin* 18 (Spring 1973): 45–81.

applied over a broad sample of industries. But the Census's efforts only apply to manufacturing industries; they are only conducted approximately every five years; and their usefulness is severely diminished in that the Census's classification does not always correlate to economic markets, in terms of either product definition or geographic boundaries. Data on individual firm's shares are even more sparse. It is perhaps not surprising, then, that most recommendations for a broadened program of DDD also propose a new administrative mechanism for gathering data and impartially determining the economic boundaries of the markets being studied. If this important chore cannot be carried out objectively, then the case for DDD based on market shares is fatally weakened.

Frank Knight once wrote that monopoly profits were simply those that were "too large" and lasted "too long."[20] As mentioned, some dissolution proposals are indeed to be triggered by the existence of high rates of return.[21] Yet, from an economic standpoint, the existence of this condition is a precarious test for antitrust actions.

Economic analysis distinguishes monopoly profit from accounting profit. Accounting profit is the difference between a firm's revenues and its costs, the latter as measured by various accounting conventions and requirements of the tax laws. Economic profit is the difference between the value of a firm's output and the value of the inputs, the latter as measured by the alternative opportunities they have foregone. Consequently, accounting profits may include a return for the bearing of risk, rents accruing to superior factors of production, disequilibrium returns due to increases in demand, innovations, decreases in factor prices, or, in the case of owner-managed firms, returns that are in fact wages or interest on the owner's own efforts or investment. In addition, a firm's expenditures on research and development and advertising may yield an intangible capital stock that accountants normally treat as a current expense. The accountants' omission of intangible capital understates the "true" capital of the enterprise and therefore overstates the rate of return

20. Frank H. Knight, "An Appraisal of Economic Change, Discussion," *American Economic Review* (Proceedings) 44 (May 1954): 63–66, at p. 65.

21. For example, the legislation proposed by Senator Philip Hart defines market power as the ability of a corporation to receive an average rate of return on net worth in excess of 15 percent over a period of five consecutive years out of the most recent seven preceding an antitrust complaint.

on equity. All of these factors would have to be subtracted from accounting profits in searching for monopoly profit.

Furthermore, economic analysis would predict a correlation between monopoly power and monopoly profits only in those product lines in which a firm had monopoly power. In multiproduct firms, the aggregate (published) profit figure would be almost meaningless because it embraces too much. Consequently, profit reporting on an individual product basis is a prerequisite to the rational use of this variable in antitrust enforcement.

The two remaining triggering variables, the firm's absolute size and the firm's price behavior, lend themselves more readily to reliable measurement. Data on firm size, for example, are obtainable from corporate accounting records and would presumably be, for most DDD contenders, already public information.

Antitrust authorities presently have access to a variety of public sources on price data. Many of these price series must be used with caution because they generally report book (or list) prices rather than actual transactions (or invoice) prices. The latter often are a shading of the former and are, of course, the more relevant data for antitrust purposes.[22] A meticulous antitrust investigation can always document price behavior with precision by examining the actual sales invoices of the firm (and its customers).

The second critical question regarding these benchmarks is whether their utilization might involve adverse side effects that outweigh any benefits from DDD. There is reason to believe that each of the first four would. All of them share a common defect. Once instituted, they would not work or perform the triggering function as intended because the firms would adapt to them. These adaptations would, in almost every instance, result in inefficient behavior.

For example, once it is recognized that any firm (or industry) that reaches a certain market share (or level of concentration) is subject to

22. Richard Posner, who advocates basing shared monopoly charges on observed price behavior, has suggested that the government be allowed to base a prima facie case on the behavior of list prices, allowing the firms the opportunity to rebut this with their own evidence of transaction prices. See his "Oligopoly and the Antitrust Laws: A Suggested Approach," *Stanford Law Review* 21 (June 1969): 1562–1606, at p. 1581–1582.

dismantling, businesses will forego aggressive competition, raise prices, or reduce product quality as this limit is approached. If the limit is on single firm shares, the leading firm would raise its prices or refuse to sell additional output as it approached the designated limit. If the triggering percentage were applied to the joint market share of the leading firms, there would be an additional incentive for collusion in order to assure that the group is not penalized by the vigorous sales activities of one of the leaders. On the other hand, knowing that the leaders cannot expand beyond a given market share without inviting antitrust action may be a stimulus to new entry into the concentrated market. And if the firm is allowed to retain its profits or market share for enough years prior to the attack, it may go ahead and behave aggressively in the interim. Once a time deadline on the duration of the established profit rates or market shares is announced, however, firms will lessen their efforts as the deadline approaches.

The same predicament exists with regard to using profits as a signal for DDD. If a rate of return above a certain level would initiate dissolution proceedings, it can be predicted with confidence that this particular level of profit will never be registered in the future. Less efficient methods of production will be adopted, managerial expenses will be increased, and advertising, marketing, and R & D costs (all readily adjustable) will be elevated to suboptimal levels in an effort to raise costs.

The implications go well beyond the mere avoidance of antitrust suits. If resources are still to flow into their most productive uses, business firms and investors will have to devise sources of information other than their published accounts to learn in which directions consumer tastes are shifting, in what markets factor costs are changing, and what divisions and firms should be contracting or expanding. Ultimately the consumer would bear the burden of the shift to this costly, somewhat sub-rosa means of gathering and exchanging economic information.

An absolute size criterion would also be anticompetitive over time. Firms that were "too large" at the time the size mandate was imposed might not behave perversely. But any firm approaching the size limit in the future would, if the DDD limit were credible, hold back. Such strategic behavior could be perverse from a competitive standpoint.

The only triggering variable among the five listed that does not have the defect of inducing anticompetitive behavior is the observance of rigid or harmonious price behavior. The threat of DDD would provide an incentive to adopt independent price strategies or to avoid signs of collusive behavior. However, as will be seen, fines are a less costly penalty and could produce the same result.

In short, there is some finite probability that structural relief will become a prominent weapon in the antitrust arsenal, a weapon that could be competently wielded in the public interest. But free market proponents should recognize that this probability is decidedly less than 1. Even granted the existence of large welfare losses due to concentrated market structures, the economic, judicial, and administrative difficulties pursuant to corporate dissolution, as well as the inefficiency inherent in some of the triggering benchmarks, weigh against the widespread use of this antitrust instrument.

7

FINES: THE EFFICIENT SOLUTION

The Coasian Framework

Chapter 5 argued that monopoly damages are reciprocal in nature. The real issue is where to place the liability for the untoward economic repercussions of anticompetitive practices. Placing the liability squarely on the antitrust violator by requiring him to pay compensation to his "victims" does not permit an efficient solution since it changes the incentives of those potentially compensated, thus generating unintended and adverse side effects. These side effects would persist even if the reparations process were costless, which it assuredly is not.

The Coasian analysis would suggest that consideration should be given to placing the liability on the consumer and then comparing the results under such a system with the results of the strict liability approach of present treble damage law. It is clear, however, that shifting the liability to the consumer with no liability placed on the monopolist would not be efficient. Furthermore, it would be equivalent to having no antitrust laws. The consumer would then bear the entire burden of damages arising from monopolistic practices. Since the consumer's surplus lost would be larger than the monopolist's profits, there is still a potential for "gains from trade." But the large numbers problem and the free rider argument dash the hope that strictly private transactions would eliminate the monopolistic market structure. It is unlikely that even the most assiduous and prudent conduct on the part of shoppers by itself would deter, for if there were always effective substitutes in the market there would be no monopoly problem. There are thus sharp limits to the benefits to be had from a completely laissez-faire approach. To achieve optimality in the Coasian sense (that is, to maximize the value of total output), *some* liability must be placed on the monopolist.

Since negotiation is impractical and perfect substitutes do not exist, consideration must be given to finding a solution through governmental action. In this case, it appears that the optimal solution is precisely the kind that Coase once suggested might prove correct in the case of other social costs. The optimal solution calls for neither compensation for damages suffered nor for allowing monopoly to persist unabated. Coase himself, in discussing another type of liability issue, suggested that in some instances the liability for damages must be *shared* in order to reach an optimal solution.[1]

But what could such a prescription mean in the context of antitrust policy? The answer is to place the liability for monopolistic behavior on *both* buyers and sellers. Under the ideal solution, the monopolistic sellers would be fined enough to cause them to cease and desist from all monopolistic behavior, but they would be exempt from paying compensation to anyone who purchased from them. Buyers as well as sellers would then share the "liability." With no potential compensation, perverse incentives and misinformation effects would be eliminated and the perplexities and costs of the reparations process would vanish.

To die-hard advocates of private enforcement, such a prescription might appear unwarranted. They might argue that increasing the amount of damages that plaintiffs could receive would at some point completely deter monopolistic behavior.[2] This increase could be accomplished by increasing the multiple of damages that is paid to successful plaintiffs to

1. R. H. Coase, "The Problem of Social Cost," *Journal of Law & Economics* 3 (October 1960): 1, reprinted in William Breit and Harold M. Hochman, *Readings in Microeconomics* 2d ed. rev. (New York: Holt, Rinehart, and Winston, 1971), p. 515. Buchanan and Stubblebine have also suggested that a bilateral approach to liability might sometimes be necessary to achieve full Pareto equilibrium. See James M. Buchanan and William Craig Stubblebine, "Externality," *Economica* 29 (n.s.) (November 1962): 371. Guido Calabresi in *The Costs of Accidents: A Legal and Economic Analysis* points out that an efficient approach to automobile liability law would stress the reciprocal nature of accidents involving both cars and pedestrians noting that "the cheapest way of avoiding costs, is often a reduction of *both* activities, walking and driving" [New Haven: Yale University Press, 1970], p. 154.

2. Gary S. Becker is a leading exemplar of this point of view. See his "Crime and Punishment: An Economic Approach," *Journal of Political Economy* 76 (March-April 1968): 169. Reprinted in Breit and Hochman, *Reading in Microeconomics,* pp. 339–369, esp. 360.

one that would lead to complete deterrence, by easing the process of successfully consummating private suits, or by a combination of the two.

Although it might at first appear that appropriately increasing the amount of damages, in deterring all monopoly, would surely eliminate the moral hazards of private actions, further examination renders this conclusion dubious. Increasing private payments to the point where monopoly is deterred would eventually eliminate the perverse incentives effect, because if no one could be damaged by monopolists there would be no damages to be avoided. In addition, an individual could not modify his behavior to increase his damage, since without monopolies there would be no monopolistic damages to be increased.

However, the amelioration of one adverse effect of a private action can be obtained in this way only by exacerbating the other. For the higher the amount of damages that could be collected, and the greater the ease with which such suits could be consummated, the greater will be the misinformation effect. As has been shown, nuisance suits are more likely to occur when a defendant cannot easily show that the claimant's charges are groundless and when the defendant predicts that he has a good chance of being found guilty. If a defendant is risk averse, and his expected payment to allegedly injured claimants is relatively large, the greater will be his desire to settle without litigation. We would predict that any attempt to deter monopolistic activity through increasing payments to plaintiffs or easing the way to their bringing and winning suits would increase the amount of misinformation that the system generates regarding the extent of monopolistic activity. Even total deterrence, then, under a system of private actions, would not be efficient deterrence because of the resources misallocated to nuisance and *in terrorem* suits. Indeed the closer the approach to total deterrence, the greater would be the extent of this misallocation.

To obviate these problems under a private actions approach, it would be necessary to consider a complicated multipronged attack on the problem. First, only unavoidable damages could merit compensation. This change would require an alteration in the present attitude of the courts toward this problem. Otherwise, the magnified perverse incentives effect would persist under a regime of compensation. But even if this effect were eliminated, the perverse incentives effect would remain unless compensation were not paid to those actually damaged. This might be accomplished through a system of entrepreneurial law firms that, in return for rewards, detected antitrust law violations. Second, even assuming that the perverse incentives effect were completely eliminated, the misinformation effect would persist. It would be greatly reduced, of course, if the law were changed so as to assign all legal fees to unsuccessful plaintiffs. If this action did not eliminate the misinformation effect, it would be necessary to impose heavy penalties upon those bringing unsuccessful suits.[3] The superiority of this approach is not persuasive, however. For one thing, such a system of penalties might dampen the enthusiasm not only of those with groundless claims but those with viable grievances as well. And even if it is assumed that the perverse incentives effect and the misinformation effect could be eliminated by these actions, there remain two seemingly incorrigible problems of a full-fledged reliance on private antitrust enforcement: (1) substantive reform of the antitrust laws would have to be undertaken so that only procompetitive actions would be brought; (2) in the event that such a system led to overenforcement of the antitrust laws, one would have to calculate an optimal tax on private enforcement in order to lower the equilibrium probability of conviction to the desired level.[4]

As a first approximation to an optimal solution, a monetary fine should be levied that would be sufficient to deter most risk averse managers and that would enable society to achieve at least the present degree of deterrence at far less cost and a greater degree of deterrence at the same cost. Given this mandatory fine, the Antitrust Division and Federal Trade Commission could then increase or decrease the amount of monopolistic activity by altering the amount of resources used in detecting and convicting antitrust violators. In other words, the antitrust authorities could adjust policy through marginal increments in the amount of investigatory and litigative activity permitted. Under public enforcement

3. We are indebted to Gary Becker for an illuminating discussion of these points with us.
4. On the general subject of private law enforcement, see Gary S. Becker and George J. Stigler, "Law Enforcement, Malfeasance, and Compensation of Enforcers," *Journal of Legal Studies* 3 (January 1974): 1.

of the antitrust laws, the optimal combination of probabilities and punish
ments would more readily be approximated. Under a private action
approach, on the other hand, it is unlikely that such an outcome coul
be obtained. The amount of resources devoted to the apprehension an
conviction of violators could only be changed through the use of th
blunt instruments of congressional legislation or court decisions, whic
could ease or hinder the bringing of private actions. With public enforce
ment, however, a change in total antitrust activity could be accomplishe
by simply changing the congressional appropriations for these agencie
and the discretionary use to which the antitrust authorities put thes
resources. This policy (permissible only through public actions) woul
thus entail faster and more predictable antitrust enforcement.

One likely criticism of a proposal to rely upon a high monetary ex
action combined with governmental control over the mechanisms tha
initiate enforcement is the argument that the antitrust authorities woul
be subject to temptations to accept bribes in lieu of bringing charge
against a violator. Since the gain to the violators is potentially greate
than that to the antitrust authorities from preventing or punishing thos
who would infringe the law, the quality of enforcement might b
lessened. The higher the fine, the greater would be the temptation t
malfeasance, and the greater would be the costs of monitoring the ant
trust authorities. However, as Becker and Stigler have demonstrated,
compensation structure that would eliminate malfeasance can be de
veloped.[5] The higher the salary paid to enforcers, the greater is the co
to them of violations of trust. An alternative would be to increase th
penalties for dishonesty. In other words, the cost of dismissal to
public law enforcer could be made greater than the gain he received fro
dishonesty.

What Do Entrepreneurs Want?

Can economic reasoning shed any light on the question of the efficienc
of fines—the remaining antitrust penalty? In other words, what kind c
fine would be appropriate and how high should it be? In order to analyz

5. Ibid.

this problem it will be necessary to examine the motivations of the entrepreneurs whose behavior these fines are presumably designed to affect. Stated in its starkest form, assuming that the entrepreneur is attempting to maximize his expected utility, then antitrust violations will occur if the expected utility from anticompetitive behavior exceeds the expected utility from competing. But the economists' term "expected utility" is a portmanteau that requires unpacking.

The entrepreneur's "expected utility" simply refers to the average or mean level of his satisfactions from his business activities. They are "expected" because he operates under conditions of uncertainty and he cannot know in advance whether he will actually realize any particular amount of profits. Only a set of probabilities is known. There are essentially three items that must be taken into account in order to predict accurately the behavior of, say, a potential cartelist. First, the entrepreneur is interested in the additional profits he will realize from joining the cartel. But he is actually interested in the present value of those profits. This value tells him how much his firm is worth. He then discounts these profits by the probability of his being detected and convicted, and by the risk of high fines he must pay, an exercise that gives him his expected value. The second item is thus the probability of detection and conviction as well as the size of the fine. This risk is part of his costs and reduces the present value of his monopoly profits and therefore the capitalized value of his enterprise. Insofar as it is a deterrent, antitrust policy works by making the present value of monopoly profits less by increasing the risk facing the potential and actual cartelist. But how much this policy will actually deter the firm from illegal behavior depends on the entrepreneur's attitude toward risk. The more averse he is to risk, the more he will be deterred by any given reduction in the present value of his monopoly profits resulting from increased risk. The more of a risk lover he happens to be, the less will he be deterred by any reduction in the present value of his monopoly profits resulting from increased risk. So the third important item in appraising any antitrust policy is the attitude of the businessman toward risk. His attitude toward risk determines the utility or satisfaction that he expects to get from his monopoly profits. And, as already noted, his expected utility from monopoly profits must be greater than his expected utility from his competitive returns before he would be willing to collude. With these functional relationships in mind, under what conditions will the entrepreneur enter a cartel or engage in monopolistic behavior?

The present value of a firm is the discounted stream of expected profits. Any increase in the financial penalties or in the probability of detection and conviction would increase the risk facing this firm. This increase would cause a rise in the firm's average costs because shareholders would insist on a higher return because the riskiness of the enterprise has increased.[6] They will sell shares, reducing the market value of the stock and increasing its yield. The increased yield indicates a higher cost of capital to the firm. Consequently the rising probability of antitrust conviction or the risk of paying higher financial penalties increases average costs and reduces the present value of the profit accruing to the firm. If the goal of antitrust activity was totally to deter this cartel, then the best policy would be to increase the risk, making the firm's average costs rise so high that the expected utility of monopoly profits would be zero. At that point there would be no incentive to collude since the expected utility of profits under competitive conditions would be the same as those under collusive conditions.

By now it should be clear that Congress can affect monopoly behavior by acting on two variables: the probability of detection and conviction and fines. For example, if society wishes to increase competition, one variable to modify would be the amount of resources devoted to the detection and conviction of anticompetitive behavior; another would be the size of the financial penalty.

There is widespread agreement that, everything else being equal, an increase in the probability of detection and conviction will decrease the number of offenses an individual will commit. Whether this decrease will be negligible or substantial, however, is open to question. There has long been a presumption among sociologists, government officials, and even businessmen that the decrease will be substantial, because, it is alleged, the severity of a sentence is less important than the likelihood that it will be imposed. In 1949, for example, Ellis Arnall, former governor of Georgia and president of the Society of Independent Motion

6. See William Fellner, "Average-Cost Pricing and the Theory of Uncertainty," *Journal of Political Economy* 56 (June 1948): 249.

Picture Producers, testified before a congressional committee to study monopoly power. He suggested that "in most criminal laws the deterrent from crime is the certainty of the punishment." But in the case of the antitrust laws, "the certainty of punishment is not a deterrent because the punishment does not amount to anything."[7] In 1961, Lee Loevinger, the chief of the Antitrust Division, repeated the conventional view:

> It is the general experience of law enforcement officials that severity of punishment is not nearly as effective a deterrent to law violation as certainty of apprehension and punishment. Increasing the severity of punishment does not aid in the detection and apprehension of violators. It is the enforcement machinery and the tools of detection and apprehension that are the indispensable weapons of law enforcement.[8]

In like fashion, when urging stronger antitrust laws, Henry Ford II stated his view that increasing the penalties would not be as effective a deterrent as greater enforcement efforts. The "threat of fairly certain detection, [and] conviction for violation would be enough to deter all but the most incorrigible offenders."[9] If these statements are correct, then a plausible argument can be made in favor of enlarging the budgets of the Antitrust Division and the Federal Trade Commission. And precisely such measures have been endorsed, recently by the Nader antitrust study group.[10] Willard Mueller, a former director of the Federal Trade Commission's Bureau of Economics, has written that "antitrust policy has never been given a fair test" because of its lean funding.[11]

7. Testimony of Ellis Arnall in U.S., Congress, House, Committee on the Judiciary, *Hearings on the Study of Monopoly Power*, 81st Cong., 1st Sess., 1949, p. 278.

8. U.S., Congress, Senate, Committee on the Judiciary, *Hearings, Legislation to Strengthen Penalties Under the Antitrust Laws*, 87th Cong., 1st Sess., 1961, p. 17.

9. Letter from Henry Ford II to Estes Kefauver, cited in *ibid.*, p. 107.

10. Mark J. Green, et al., *The Closed Enterprise System* (New York: Grossman Publishers, 1972), pp. 129–130. Arguing that the present budget of the Antitrust Division is "absurdly too small," the study group recommended an increase from the present budget of $12 million to "at least $100 million," p. 130.

11. Willard F. Mueller, *A Primer On Monopoly and Competition* (New York: Random House, 1970), p. 177.

As a second alternative, society could act upon the variable of fines by increasing their magnitude. Chapter 3 noted a number of proposals to do just that.[12] However, the appropriate choice or "mix" between the level of the fine and probability of detection and conviction depends upon the precise extent to which manipulating them will deter monopolistic behavior. And this deterrence is a direct function of the attitude of the businessman toward risk. Consequently it is now necessary to examine the meaning of risk preference as it relates to managerial behavior.

Risk Preference and Antitrust Policy

An illustration comparing a given large loss with a given smaller loss will prove instructive in clarifying the meaning of risk preference. Assume that the large loss is ten times the smaller loss. The expected value of these two losses is said to be equal if the probability of the occurrence of the small loss is ten times as great as that of the large loss. However, although the expected values are the same, individuals may have different expected disutilities from these losses depending upon their attitudes toward risk. The risk averse person will prefer the large probability of the small loss to the small probability of the large loss. The risk preferrer, on the other hand, will prefer the small probability of the large loss to the larger probability of the smaller loss. More technically, for the risk averse person the disutility of the larger loss is more than ten times as great as the disutility of the smaller loss. For the risk preferrer, the larger loss disutility is less than ten times that of the smaller loss.

Let us apply this risk attitude analysis to our antitrust policy problem of choosing between a primarily fine-oriented and a primarily detection-oriented deterrence system. Assume that the enforcement agencies are considering two alternative proposals. The first calls for both the imposition of a higher fine on convicted antitrust violators and a reduction in the amount of resources going into detection and conviction. The second calls for reducing the financial penalties but also for increasing the resources devoted to enforcement, thereby causing an increase in

12. See pp. 55–62 supra.

the probability of detection and conviction. Let us assume further that the high financial penalty is ten times the lower penalty, but that because of the difference in the quantity of resources devoted to enforcement, the probability of being required to pay the lower penalty is ten times as great as the probability of being required to pay the high penalty. Based on these assumptions, the expected value of monopoly profits under either proposal is the same. The businessman's expected utility from antitrust violations, however, will vary depending upon his attitude toward risk. The risk averse manager's attitudes will lead him to practice more collusion under the policy involving the larger probability of paying the smaller financial penalty. The risk preferrer, on the other hand, will practice more collusion under the policy involving the smaller probability of the large penalty.

The indifference maps of figure 4 provide graphic illustration of the attitudes of both a risk preferrer and a risk averter. On the horizontal axes of panels A and B is measured the probability of detection and conviction of antitrust violations. On the vertical axes is measured fines paid when the firm is apprehended and convicted of restraints of trade.[13] Unlike relative magnitudes in the usual construction of such diagrams, the magnitudes measured on each axis become smaller as they move away from the origin. The indifference curves depicted will be called "iso-expected utility" curves. They show for a given businessman combinations of antitrust policies associated with a particular expected utility from monopoly profits. A movement along any curve indicates the amount by which a decrease in the use of one policy instrument must be compensated by an increase in employment of the other instrument in order for a given businessman to maintain a given degree of utility from monopolistic activity. As the businessman moves out to higher iso-expected utility curves—that is, as he moves further away from the origin—the greater satisfaction that he can achieve from monopoly profits will encourage him to engage in more anticompetitive behavior.

13. The magnitude of fines is independent of the probability of conviction and detection. Congress could increase the fines and not vote any additional resources to the enforcement agencies. Furthermore, increased fines provide no significant inducement to private parties either to prosecute or to inform the government of antitrust violations.

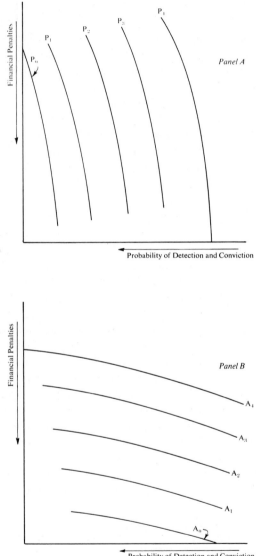

Figure 4

A preliminary issue that figure 4 can help illuminate is the inefficiency of incarceration as an antitrust weapon. In chapter 3 this penalty was seen to have little deterrent effect because of the paucity of its use, an understandable situation given the reluctance of judges and juries to believe either that antitrust violators merit jail or that the chief corporate culprits have been identified. But the analysis in this chapter allows one to go beyond such a purely pragmatic consideration. For if the horizontal axis of figure 4 is understood as depicting incarceration in terms of the length of the sentence (rather than probability of detection and conviction), the indifference curves would then represent a plausible trade-off between financial penalties and time to be served in jail. In other words, the geometry brings out clearly that there is some marginal rate of substitution between financial penalties and *any* other penalty, including jails, which means that the jail penalty, like any other penalty, can always be collapsed into its monetary equivalent. Thus the inefficiency of the jail penalty can be easily seen. For any given period of time spent in jail, there is some fine capable of securing the same deterrent effect. However, since the size of a fine can be changed without the expenditure of additional resources, while increased use of incarceration always involves greater costs to society, incarceration is an inferior penalty. Whenever any penalty can give the same amount of deterrence at less cost, or additional deterrence for the same cost, that option is economically superior.

More important, this geometrical construct can be used to see the implications of managerial risk attitudes in the design of antitrust policy. Panel A depicts the case in which the manager is a risk preferrer. His indifference curves indicate that a relatively small reduction in the probability of apprehension and conviction must be compensated by a relatively large increase in financial penalties in order for him to maintain any given degree of expected utility from his monopolistic behavior. Precisely the opposite attitude is depicted in panel B, which illustrates the case of a risk averse manager. In this case, a relatively large reduction in the probability of detection and conviction needs to be compensated by only a relatively small increase in penalties in order to maintain any given expected utility.

The implications of attitudes toward risk for antitrust policy can be illustrated by superimposing the expected utility indifference curves of the risk preferrer (the curves depicted as P) on those of the risk averter (the curves depicted as A), as is done in figure 5. Assume that in terms of current expenditures of resources, antitrust policy places society at point Q, where the A_3 indifference curve of the risk averter cuts curve P_3 of the risk preferrer. The line KL passes through point Q and is drawn as an iso-expected value curve. By definition, any movement along KL leaves constant the expected value of the monopolist's profits, with any change in the financial penalty exactly compensated in terms of expected value by an opposite change in the probability of detection and conviction. The iso-expected value curve, a rectangular hyperbola, also represents the iso-expected utility curve of a risk-neutral businessman, a businessman who has no preference, say, between a 10 percent probability of a $10 loss and a 100 percent probability of a $1 loss. KL can thus be thought of as the line that divides risk preference from risk aversion.[14] The slopes of iso-expected utility curves at each point of intersection with KL are greater or less than the slope of KL, depending upon whether they represent risk preferrers or risk averters.

If one were to start at point Q on KL and were to allow both P and A to design any antitrust policy they wished, with the only constraint being that the expected value of their monopoly profits would have to remain constant, one would expect each businessman to travel up or down the iso-expected value curve KL until he reached his highest iso-expected

14. That criminals are risk neutral (i.e., that line KL accurately depicts their psychology) is implicitly assumed by Gordon Tullock. In discussing the question of whether the severity of the penalty or the certainty of punishment is more important in deterring criminal behavior, Tullock stated his opinion that "this is not a very important question. Suppose a potential criminal has a choice between two punishment systems: One gives each person who commits burglary a one-in-100 chance of serving one year in prison; in the other there is a one-in-1,000 chance of serving 10 years. It is not obvious to me that burglars would be very differently affected by these two punishment systems, although in one case there is a heavy sentence with a low probability of conviction, and in the other a lighter sentence with a higher probability of conviction." See Gordon Tullock, "Does Punishment Deter Crime?" *The Public Interest* 36 (Summer 1974): 103–107. Our indifference curve analysis makes clear, however, that the probability that a potential burglar would commit more crime under one or the other of these two systems depends on his attitude toward risk.

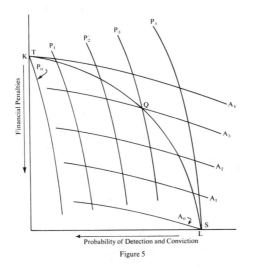

Figure 5

utility indifference curve. In figure 5, the risk averter reaches his highest indifference curve at point T, while the risk preferrer reaches his highest expected utility at point S. Point T represents relatively low monetary losses with a high likelihood of detection, while point S represents relatively high losses with a low probability of detection.

Of course, in reality both risk averse and risk loving managers must adjust their behavior to the same antitrust policy. The law cannot allow each of them to choose the combination he prefers under the constraint of a specific expected value of monopoly profits. With an initial policy placing them both at point Q, a new policy that would place them both at point S would move the risk preferrer to a higher indifference curve than he was on at point Q, but it would move the risk averter to a lower curve than *he* was on at point Q. By moving to point S, therefore, the expected utility of the risk lover would rise relative to that of the risk averter. The risk preferrer would engage in or "demand" more anticompetitive collusion, boycotts, mergers, and the like. He will receive more satisfaction from his monopoly profits when the probability of detection is low and the financial penalties high. On the other hand, the risk averter at point S will choose business practices and policies that involve less monopolistic activity because such activity offers him less expected utility.

With any given antitrust enforcement policy, then, the degree of monopoly in the economy depends on whether managerial classes consist mainly of risk preferrers or risk averters. Changes in the risk attitudes of the managing classes may demand corresponding changes in antitrust policies. It is therefore highly pertinent to examine the development of the risk attitudes of American business management since the enactment of the Sherman Act.[15]

The Psychology of Managers and Its Implications for Antitrust Policy

There is considerable evidence that today's business management is distinctly more cautious than its late nineteenth-century counterpart; furthermore, this tendency toward greater risk aversion appears to be centered in the nation's oligopolies, those firms most subject to antitrust scrutiny. Joseph Schumpeter and Robert Aaron Gordon were among the earliest observers of this attitudinal change.[16] Schumpeter's sweeping description of capitalism, in its very success, smothering and making obsolete the entrepreneurial spirit dovetails with Gordon's careful investigation of large enterprise management. Gordon argued that the desire for security is "very probably . . . stronger among the leading executives of large and mature concerns than it was among an earlier generation of 'big' businessmen."[17]

---

15. In enacting the Sherman Act, Congress in all likelihood did not explicitly or implicitly consider the risk attitudes of American businessmen. The earlier discussion of legislative history indicated that such matters were at best peripheral to the consideration of the legislation. Nevertheless, the ultimate effectiveness of the antitrust laws is in fact intimately related to management's attitudes toward risk.

16. Robert A. Gordon, *Business Leadership in the Large Corporation* (Washington: The Brookings Institution, 1945), pp. 271–351; Joseph A. Schumpeter, *Capitalism, Socialism, and Democracy,* 3d ed. (New York: Harper, 1950), pp. 121–163.

17. Robert A. Gordon, *Business Leadership,* p. 283. See also pp. 310–311.

Since Schumpeter and Gordon made their observations, other economists have also argued convincingly that American business prudence has sharply increased in recent decades. Both Robin Marris and John Kenneth Galbraith contend that control of large enterprises has passed from the individualistic entrepreneur to the organization-minded, group-oriented manager who is highly concerned with minimizing risk and uncertainty.[18] In the Galbraith-Marris corporate world, concern for individual and corporate security acts as an overriding constraint on desires for growth and profits:

> Today, when one young executive describes another as a "good businessman", more often than not he does not mean . . . a man with a good nose for profits, but rather a man who keeps his records in order, his staff contented, his contacts active and his pipelines filled; . . . not rash, but not suffering from indecision; a good committee man who knows both when to open his mouth and when to keep it shut.[19]

The use of complex decision theory and organization theory has led other economists similarly to conclude that contemporary management wishes to avoid risk and uncertainty.[20] These analysts portray a hired management interested not solely in maximizing profits but rather

18. John Kenneth Galbraith, *The New Industrial State,* 2d ed. rev. (Boston: Houghton-Mifflin, 1971), pp. 11–178; Robin Marris, *The Economic Theory of "Managerial" Capitalism* (New York: Free Press of Glencoe, 1964), pp. 1–109, 204–288.

19. Robin Marris, *Economic Theory of "Managerial" Capitalism;* pp. 57–58. Galbraith's description is consistent with Marris's view: "These characteristics [of individualistic entrepreneurial behavior] are not readily reconciled with the requirements of the technostructure. Not indifference but sensitivity to others, not individualism but accommodation to organization, not competition but intimate and continuing cooperation are the prime requirements for group action. . . . The assertion of competitive individualism . . . to the extent that it is still encountered, is ceremonial, traditional or a manifestation of personal vanity and . . . self delusion" (Galbraith, *The New Industrial State,* at 92–93).

20. See, for example, Kenneth E. Boulding, *A Reconstruction of Economics* (New York: Wiley, 1950); Richard M. Cyert and James G. March, *A Behavioral Theory of the Firm* (Englewood Cliffs, N.J.: Prentice-Hall, 1963), pp. 118–119; Herbert A. Simon, "Theories of Decision-Making in Economics and Behavioral Science," *American Economic Review* 49 (June 1959): 253.

in pursuing a variety of goals; they describe a management geared to "homeostatic" business conduct rather than impetuous, swashbuckling strategies. According to many economists, the risk attitudes of contemporary management are well summarized by Sir J. R. Hicks's observation mentioned earlier: "The best of all . . . profits is a quiet life."[21]

Observers in other disciplines have also noticed the changed risk attitude of contemporary management. William Whyte has argued that the displacement of the Protestant Ethic by the Social Ethic has led to the professionalization of management, strict pressures to conform, and constraints on individual expression.[22] Political scientist Antony Jay has compared the large corporation with the large state, arguing that both generate strong pressures to maintain the status quo. Jay believes that any risky moves that are made by today's management are aberrations, atypical phenomena that have little connection with the risk attitudes of management in general.[23]

Observers find, then, that modern enterprise lacks the Carnegies, Fricks, and Firestones of an earlier era. Such entrepreneurs have been displaced during a gradual evolution propelled by such factors as increasing education, changes in the social environment of business, the steady separation of ownership from control in large corporate enterprises, the "technique orientation" and conformity that seem to characterize business education, and perhaps the very nature of bureaucracy itself. These factors have caused the risk preferrers of the late nineteenth century to become the risk avoiders of the current era.

The implications of this attitudinal change for antitrust policy are clear. Policy designers should be highly sensitive to this change in risk attitude, realizing that a risk averse management is more likely to be deterred by high financial penalties than by a high probability of detection and conviction with accompanying penalties that are not so

21. J. R. Hicks, "Annual Survey of Economic Theory: The Theory of Monopoly," *Econometrica* 3 (January 1935): 1, 8.

22. William H. Whyte, Jr., *The Organization Man* (New York: Simon and Schuster, 1956), pp. 18–22.

23. Antony Jay, *Management and Machiavelli* (New York: Holt, Rinehart, and Winston, 1967), esp. pp. 189–198.

severe. Thus, the deterrent benefits of a policy of increased fines far outweigh the deterrent benefits of expending additional enforcement resources.

Potential Objections to Raising Fines

Even given the relative deterrent benefits of increasing fines as opposed to increasing enforcement efforts, potential objections to a fine-oriented system still remain. First, it could be argued that judges and juries would be substantially less likely to convict a violator if such a conviction demanded a significantly higher fine. If so, an increased fine, even if enforcement efforts remained constant, would result in a decrease in the proportion of antitrust violators who are convicted. The decrease, the argument would assert, would result in the reduction of moral inhibitions against engaging in anticompetitive behavior. As a consequence, antitrust violations would increase, even if management is risk averse and therefore initially inclined to avoid any flirtation with violation because of the increased penalties. This objection to a system based on higher fines rests on the belief that the moral, educative force of law is critical in influencing behavior and that to the extent that punishment occurs less frequently, the law's moral force is weakened.[24] Punishment, it is argued, greatly reinforces society's condemnation of inappropriate behavior. Hence high fines that are seldom imposed would lead in the long run to more, rather than less, monopolistic behavior because the moral inhibitions against such behavior would be weakened.

However convincing this objection to a fine-oriented system appears at first glance, on closer examination it has two critical weaknesses. First, it is far from inevitable that statutory provisions for higher fines, even if mandatory, would impel judges and juries to punish fewer antitrust violators. Legislation that increased fines while eliminating private damage suits, for example, would clearly show that Congress intended

24. See, for example, Johs Andenaes, "General Prevention—Illusion or Reality?" *Journal of Criminal Law, Criminology, and Police Science* 43 (May-June 1952): 176.

the fine increase to be comprehensively implemented; this demonstrated intent could be expected to influence judges and juries. These individuals would probably have a greater tendency to fine antitrust violations when assured that private treble damage actions would not follow. Furthermore, judges and perhaps juries could be expected to recognize that, with relatively fewer investigative resources devoted to punishing anticompetitive behavior, fines would carry a greater deterrent burden.

Second, even if one ignores the real possibility that the increased moral inhibitions accompanying heightened financial penalties may in themselves compensate for the moral inhibitions lost by a decrease in the frequency of enforcement, the moral force argument is not persuasive. It assumes that the decision to engage in unlawful behavior is made largely on the basis of an individual's personal moral code. It is more likely, however, that in the area of antitrust deterrence, the attitude of managers toward risk is far more important than any of their moral attitudes, and that antitrust policy will be more effective in deterring illegal behavior if it takes more account of the former than the latter. In consequence, a fine-oriented system would produce less, rather than more, monopolistic behavior. Until attitudes of business management toward risk change, there is no reason to expect that these risk averse managers would ever return to the monopolistic behavior once prevalent in society. Surely the moral inhibitions against such behavior—and perhaps against all illegal behavior—would be reinforced, rather than weakened.

A second potential objection to an increase in fines is that other less tangible disadvantages might accompany it. For example, such an increase might augment the sense of inequity fostered by a system that penalized some but not all violators. The equity in an after-the-fact sense (ex post equity), which is involved whenever some violators of a law are punished and others allowed to go free, decreases as the potential punishment increases. However, to achieve complete ex post equity in antitrust enforcement would entail the apprehension and punishment of all lawbreakers, an employment of resources that would clearly be too costly from the point of view of economic efficiency. At some point a balance must be struck. The crucial question is: how much is society willing to give up to achieve ex post equity?

The answer to this question should be at least partially determined by the amount of equity in the before-the-fact sense (ex ante equity)[25] that exists in the system under examination. Whatever the ex post equity in a fine-oriented system, the ex ante equity in such a system is potentially close to perfect. Each risk preferrer who cold-bloodedly decides to violate the law and enter a cartel could be made to have the same probability of being caught as anyone else. In terms of the government's enforcement efforts, each individual violator could have an equal chance of actually paying the fine. So long as the chances of being detected are equalized at the start under a clear set of rules, perfect ex ante equity can prevail. The existence of this almost perfect ex ante equity, combined with the high costs of achieving additional ex post equity, seems to indicate that a high fine system would not unduly disturb most persons' sense of justice.

Other drawbacks of an increase in fines may, however, be more significant. First, it may be that a high fine, if it represents a sum far in excess of the amount of damage done by a given antitrust violation, will also infringe on most persons' sense of justice. Furthermore, extremely high fines could cause the collapse of businesses that have at least the potential of making substantial contributions to the national economy.

Both of these considerations, however, rather than demanding that fines not be raised at all, simply indicate that there is some ceiling above which they should not go. As applied to many American businesses, the current fine structure certainly does not exceed that ceiling. The Sherman Act's maximum $1 million fine would be only an annoyance for many large firms. Nevertheless, the fact that there is a level of fines beyond which marginal costs begin to be greater than marginal

25. The distinction between ex ante and ex post equity is that of Mark V. Pauly and Thomas D. Willett. See Pauly and Willett, "Two Concepts of Equity and Their Implications for Public Policy," *Social Science Quarterly* 53 (June 1972): 8.

benefits should be kept in mind in designing a specific proposal for a
fine-oriented system.

The Fine: A Suggested Approach

It should be clear from this discussion that an absolute monetary exaction should not be set by statute for every antitrust violator. An absolute fine level that might be an enormous deterrent for small firms might
not deter larger firms from anticompetitive activity. The ideal fine
should be large enough in the case of each individual firm to make its
management unlikely to violate the antitrust laws, but it should not
be so large as to cause a violator to go out of business or to offend the
American sense of equity. Thus one must think in terms of fines based
on proportions rather than on absolute amounts. The determination
and application of these proportions should result in a fine that would
"hurt" each firm just enough to deter a risk averse manager.

Four possible measures of a firm's "ability to pay" come to mind.
In the case of the first standard, managerial salaries, fines would be
assessed against the managers themselves. If the other three measures—sales, assets, and profits—were used, the fines would be assessed
against the violating firms.

Levying fines on managers themselves would not be without advantages. While economists are no longer particularly prone to emphasize the separation of ownership and control in large corporations,
some managers' actions may still be insulated from stockholder control and reprisals. These managers may not be as much deterred by
a potential fine on their companies' sales, assets, or profits as by the
prospect of losing a percentage of their own salaries. Consequently,
there is a great temptation to fine directly the businessman engaged
in the illegal activity. If accomplished, this sort of fine would seem not
only to effectuate solid deterrence but also to constitute an equitable
incidence of the fine. A manager willfully engaging in anticompetitive
behavior should not be able to use a corporate shield to escape
punishment.

Two factors, however, militate against levying a proportional fine upon managerial salaries. First, as noted in chapter 3, the task of clearly identifying those responsible for anticompetitive behavior, especially in large corporations, might be excessively difficult;[26] managers would be encouraged to develop very subtle methods of concealing the origins of anticompetitive behavior so that responsibility for the behavior could not be traced to them. A fine based on salaries could thus fall on those not responsible for the illegal activity. Indeed, judges, unsure that imposed fines would fall upon the real violators, might be reluctant to impose fines high enough actually to deter. As in the case of the imprisonment penalty, convictions might be even fewer if such fines were mandatory.

Second, the gains to be had from anticompetitive behavior are frequently so large relative to the salaries of the managers involved that boards of directors would find it tempting to arrange for hidden side payments as "bribes" to management to engage in violations of the antitrust laws. With potentially huge rewards to be gained from anticompetitive action, even a 100 percent fine on salaries would constitute a small amount relative to the potential monopoly gains to the firm. The existence of such potential "gains from trade" would clearly invite the development of means to circumvent the fine structure. Thus, although in an abstract sense levying fines on managers' salaries would unquestionably be an effective deterrent, practical problems of implementation would seem to dictate that the use of such a standard be rejected.

The other three standards impose fines on the violating firms themselves. The sales figure standard has the advantage of being the least susceptible to illegal manipulation. This fact may have led a recent study group to recommend that violations of the Sherman Act be

26. Reflecting on his hearings on the electrical equipment cartel of the late 1950s, Senator Estes Kefauver wrote: "[I]t has been found that many times, top corporate executives 'wink' at criminal antitrust violations going on right under their noses. Rather than assure that the antitrust laws were being obeyed by their subordinates, such executives take great pains to make certain they have no 'knowledge' of any illegal activities." Press release of Senator Estes Kefauver, July 13, 1961, quoted in "Increasing Community Control over Corporate Crime —A Problem in the Law of Sanctions," *Yale Law Journal* 71 (December 1961): 280, 303 n. 71. See also pp. 297, 302.

punished by fines equal to a percentage of the violator's sales.[27] However, the benefits of using a sales standard are more than offset by the
disproportionately heavy impact that a fine on sales would have upon
some firms. Firms with low profits/sales ratios would be hurt far
more than those with high profits/sales ratios. In fact, a percentage
fine in the range of 1 to 5 percent of sales, which could cause a retailing firm with a high inventory turnover to go out of business, might be
easily endured by many manufacturing firms. The deterrent value,
equity, and destructive potential of a fine based on sales, then, would
fluctuate so widely with the character of the violating firm that the
sales standard should be rejected.

Basing the fine on assets would produce the same problem of
widely varying impacts. Upon conviction for identical offenses, firms
with low profits/assets ratios would in effect pay greater fines than
firms with high ratios. Fines more than adequate to deter anticompetitive behavior in manufacturing firms (in which there is large investment in durable capital) might not dissuade the management of
retailing or other merchandising enterprises with relatively few assets.
In addition, the fact that varying depreciation methods in different
industries exert a significant effect on the asset figure further reduces its
usefulness as a peg upon which to hang the fine structure.[28]

A firm's profits constitute a far more desirable standard for the imposition of fines than either sales or assets. The profit standard would
go further than either of the other two toward providing a constant
impact, regardless of the sales-assets structures of the firms that are
potential violators. Specifically, we suggest that antitrust violations be
penalized by a mandatory fine of 25 percent of the firm's pretax profits for every year of anticompetitive activity.[29] Government tax re-

27. Green, *The Closed Enterprise System,* p. 175. The basic proposal of this
Nader study group was a fine ranging from 1 percent to 10 percent of the violating firm's sales (during the time of the violation) for the first offense and 5
percent to 10 percent of sales for a second violation within a five-year period.
28. Moreover, during a time of inflation, a fine based on assets might impose
greater hardships on new firms than on old ones since the older firms are more
likely to have their assets undervalued.
29. Under current antitrust doctrine, the penalty of the fine is used only in
criminal cases. Since we are also proposing the use of fines as a deterrent to
what have been considered civil violations (such as illegal tying arrangements),

turns would provide a very convenient measure by which to determine the relevant profit figure.

The 25 percent figure is not to be taken as either an estimate of the firm's profits attributable to its antitrust violation or an estimate of the misallocative damage done to society by the firm's anticompetitive activity.[30] Rather than being concerned with compensation, our proposal is directed toward deterrence. The 25 percent figure is not sacrosanct, but it does represent our judgment of a penalty that would deter in an evenhanded fashion. Even a management relatively isolated from its firm's owners would feel the impact from a fine of this magnitude. The experience of lower stock prices, greater difficulties in attracting funds, and an increased probability of a takeover bid would be unpleasant consequences of such a fine. The figure of 25 percent would, on the other hand, not seem so high as to cause violators to go out of business, nor so onerous as to offend most persons' sense of equity. If experience with this percentage finds the antitrust authorities still uncovering frequent violations, Congress could increase it until anticompetitive behavior became rare.

There are, of course, some difficulties in basing the fine on a percentage of company profits. Economists have long noted the inability of current accounting practices to reflect costs rationally and consistently; the vagaries of cost accounting are necessarily reflected in the profit residual. Two problems result. First, a fine on profits may have some disproportionate effects due to different accounting practices among firms and across industries. Second, the malleability of cost figures, coupled with a potential fine on profits, gives management added incentive to hide profits. For example, a firm may have op-

---

we see no need to retain the civil-criminal distinction and would prefer that all antitrust cases be civil ones. Discussions with lawyers have persuaded us that if all antitrust cases were criminal, convictions for heretofore civil violations (such as tying) would be difficult to obtain because the criminal conviction has such an odious connotation. The imposition of fines in civil cases is not unusual—it is a common penalty, for example, for federal tax violations. On the importance of stressing the civil nature of antitrust, see the illuminating discussion by Victor Kramer, "Comment, Criminal Prosecutions For Violations of the Sherman Act: In Search of a Policy," *Georgetown Law Journal* 48 (Spring 1960): 530–542.

30. Chapter 8 shows that the present state of economic knowledge does not enable these estimations to be made with confidence.

portunities to engage in activities providing attractive tax shelters. If there were a 25 percent fine on profits, such tax shelters would benefit a firm not only by providing tax savings but also by assuring lower antitrust fines.[31] However, insofar as these problems are deemed substantial, they could be addressed by devising regulations that would use income tax profit figures not as a final base from which to compute antitrust penalties but rather as a starting point for computations.[32]

This recommendation might seem to impose an inappropriately heavy burden on multidivision firms, because the proposed fine is based on a given firm's aggregate profits even though a particular antitrust violation might have been perpetrated by only one of the company's divisions. But determining the corporate profit levels attributable only to the product line where the antitrust violation has occurred could be made extremely difficult through the use of accounting practices that obscured the source of the firm's profits. Moreover, huge multidivision firms, with many sources of profit, would probably not be "hurt" or deterred by the threat of losing a portion of profits in only one division. Furthermore, imposing even relatively frequent but relatively low fines on the profits of single divisions of conglomerates would have particularly little deterrent effect if, as concluded earlier, management is generally risk averse, and if the size and diversity of the enterprise makes the incidence of such fines more or less statistically predictable.

A final difficulty with a proportional standard is that it seems to preclude making adjustments at the margin. A firm engaging in collusive behavior in only one of its divisions, it might be argued, could lose its incentive to be honest in the economic activities of its other divisions when the penalty for violations of the antitrust laws in only one product line would be a fine that took a specific proportion of all

31. This problem should not be overemphasized. It is unlikely that our proposal would cause corporations to engage in much more tax-sheltered activity. Already existing inducements to minimize taxable income have probably exhausted concealment options.

32. Incremental concealment of profits could if necessary be made less appealing by adjusting the profit figure for antitrust penalty purposes so as to take into account returns that are otherwise hidden through sheltering devices. Firms would then be fined on the basis of an adjusted profit figure.

profits made in all product lines. This objection might suggest the appropriateness of a progressive fine. After all, a progressive fine would give a potential violator less incentive to try to maximize the amount of profits from illegal corporate activity. Further reflection indicates, however, that even with a proportional fine incentives exist to reduce the amount of profits earned from willfully violating the antitrust laws. The expected value of the fine goes up *pari passu* with increasing amounts of illegal activity, since the more any firm engages in such behavior, the more likely are the prospects of its detection and conviction. The situation facing the firm's management is analogous to that faced by a person at a cocktail party who must decide whether to chance driving home under the influence of alcohol. Since the fine for drunk driving is a flat amount regardless of the number of miles driven while intoxicated, it might at first appear that the individual would make the same decision regardless of the number of miles that would have to be driven to reach home. But clearly that is wrong. The probability of detection, and therefore the expected value of the fine, is greater the further the distance to be driven. So adjustments at the margin are made even under a flat rate fine.

The benefits of determining antitrust fines by a profit standard, then, outweigh the costs of using that standard. Considerations of efficiency, ease of administration, and equity together compel the judgment that the profit standard is the most desirable of the four options that have been analyzed here.

Given the general risk aversion of American management, it is more efficient to deter antitrust violations by heavy reliance on financial penalties. In advocating reliance on a single penalty instead of a host of weapons and in recommending the elimination of private damage suits, a mechanism that has been called the "strongest pillar of antitrust,"[33] we are not, we stress, calling for a weakening of the antitrust laws. On the contrary, we are convinced that more discouragement of anticompetitive behavior is needed. But economic analysis involves

33. L. Loevinger, "Private Action—The Strongest Pillar of Antitrust," *Antitrust Bulletin* 3 (March-April 1958): 167.

considering both the benefits and the costs of using the available anti-trust matériel. Thus we do not follow the altogether too common tendency of antitrust literature to simply recommend more of every-thing—more fines, longer jail terms, bigger government enforcement budgets, enlarged rules of standing, easier access to the courts—with little discussion of the relative efficiencies and costs of these alter-natives.

8

PUBLIC ENFORCEMENT AND
ECONOMIC EFFICIENCY

The solution to the problem of efficient antitrust enforcement is the replacement of the present reparations-induced private action system by public enforcement armed with the single device of an optimal fine. The perceptive reader may, however, have raised certain questions about the efficiency of public enforcement and the equity of eliminating reparations. Some of the possible questions are: (1) Would the perverse incentives effect and misinformation effect be operative upon the staffs of the Federal Trade Commission and the Antitrust Division? (2) Even in the absence of these effects at the enforcement level, are not government agencies subject to political pressures that abuse or subvert public enforcement efforts and that would not be present at the private level? (3) Do government agencies have an ability to ferret out antitrust violators comparable with that of private parties and would this ability be hindered by the elimination of private suits? (4) Even granting the efficiency merits of public actions, are there not equity arguments that dictate a reparations-oriented mode of antitrust enforcement? (5) Would the extension of class action suits not make private enforcement more efficient by eliminating many individual plaintiffs and thereby conserving judicial resources? (6) Do the moral hazard implications of private antitrust enforcement apply to all private actions in tort law where injury and compensation are issues? Let us deal with each of these questions in turn.

To answer the first two questions definitively would require a theory of bureaucratic behavior as thorough and precise as the theory of markets. Unfortunately, no such theory exists. Some promising theoretical beginnings that have been made concerning the behavior of bureaucracies note how internal bureaucratic incentives and external political pressures might destroy the enforcement process.[1] Notwithstanding these pressures, the fact remains that malfeasance is greater when a reward is directly pecuniary, as it is in private actions, than when enticement is in the form of nonpecuniary emoluments and fringe benefits, as is usually the case in government. Moreover, although the cop on the beat may be thought vulnerable to bribes because he has day-to-day contact with potential law violators, antitrust typically involves nonrepetitive violations and consequently the potential for malfeasance by antitrust officials is reduced.[2] In addition, while a government trust-buster might propose a suit designed only to bring him notoriety and fame (but probably not fortune), such a proposal within the government must at least pass the scrutiny of the agency's evaluation section and (increasingly) the agency's economists.[3] No comparable review or evaluation exists in the private sector.

Economists who are critical of government antitrust enforcement usually base their criticisms not upon any perverse incentives existing within the agencies (a charge they frequently level at regulatory agencies, but upon what they see as laws and decisions that enable inappropriate cases to be brought and won. This objection, however, holds for suits brought privately as well. Indeed, since the potential for so many more such suits exists in the private sector, this criticism is perhaps even more applicable there.

There can be no doubt that antitrust developments in the public sector receive far more scrutiny than private suits. Of the 7,500 private

1. See Gordon Tullock, *The Politics of Bureaucracy* (Washington: Public Affairs Press, 1965); Anthony Downs, *Inside Bureaucracy* (Boston: Little, Brown, 1967); William A. Niskanen, Jr., *Bureaucracy and Representative Government* (Chicago: Aldine, 1971).

2. Gary S. Becker and George J. Stigler, "Law Enforcement, Malfeasance, and Compensation of Enforcers," *Journal of Legal Studies* 3 (January 1974): 1.

3. The Antitrust Division established an office of policy planning and an evaluation section in 1963. A comparable office exists in the Federal Trade Commission, though in the FTC the economics bureau has increasingly served an evaluative function. Recently the Antitrust Division has increased its staff of economists significantly in order to conduct industry-by-industry investigations, ranking the importance of each industry and assessing the impact on the economy of monopolistic practices in each. See "Antitrust Reorganizes for More Action," *Business Week,* November 10, 1973, pp. 142–146.

suits brought in the 1963–1972 period, over 70.5 percent were settled even before the pretrial process and those litigated avoided the spotlight focused on government antitrust suits. While the facts behind government negotiations and out-of-court settlements with defendants are often hard to learn,[4] the nature of such negotiations in the private sector are almost completely unknown. The Administrative Office of the United States Courts keeps no public records relating to the resolution of non-litigated private actions, and there is no agency from which such data can be obtained. The implications of this divergence in public scrutiny are obvious: without gainsaying the potential for moral hazard and political influence in the public sector, the attention this sector receives and the extensive factual knowledge about its antitrust operations make it far less likely that untoward behavior exists here than is the case in the private sector.

This is not to say that the government antitrust agencies always choose cases rationally, after careful evaluation and screening, or that these agencies are free from political pressure. Such propositions would not be accurate. But in spite of the institutional impediments to rational enforcement found in government agencies, there is at least a review process, a far closer scrutiny by the press and academic community, and an imperfect (but still available) forum for complaining and criticizing the cases selected and their resolution. No similar forum exists for monitoring the selection and resolution of private suits.

The third question is whether government agencies have an ability to detect and convict antitrust violators comparable to that found in the private sector. There is no doubt that the private antitrust bar, whose stake is high, can mobilize impressive litigative skills and devices. Plaintiffs' efforts in the electrical equipment suits testify to the wealth of

4. In 1961, the attorney general announced that proposed consent judgments in government antitrust suits would be filed in court for at least thirty days before they became effective. This procedure allows some opportunity for review and criticism of government settlements. *Antitrust developments: 1955–1968, A Supplement to the Report of the Attorney General's National Committee to Study the Antitrust Laws* (Chicago; American Bar Association, 1968), pp. 228–229. The passage of S. 782, the Antitrust Procedures and Penalties Act, which opens consent decree negotiations to wider judicial and public scrutiny, is an admirable effort to further illuminate the consent decree process. Of course, it applies to only the government antitrust plaintiff.

legal devices available to the private bar to gather evidence and successfully prosecute blue-chip corporations.[5] In fact, in one monopoly suit, the Antitrust Division claimed that its own prosecution efforts would be handicapped if it were deprived of the evidence gathered in a concurrent private monopoly suit against the same defendant.[6]

Such illustrations do not reveal a true picture. The typical situation is still for the private plaintiff to enter antitrust litigation only after a government agency has already secured a conviction against the defendant on an antitrust charge. The comparative advantage of the private plaintiff (and the private plaintiff bar) is not in detecting and convicting antitrust violators but rather in litigating the questions of standing to sue and the estimation of damages (questions that would become moot under a system of fines).

If a private party files an antitrust complaint, the private plaintiff, under the Federal Rules of Civil Procedure, can require the production of defendant's documents, compel the answer of interrogatories, and take depositions in an effort to make his case. In this domain, the private plaintiff has available the same legal weapons as the government enforcement agency. In fact, the liberalization of pretrial discovery rules has aided both the government and the private plaintiff.[7]

Notwithstanding the existence of this potent collection of instruments available to private enforcers of the antitrust laws, the private sector still does not have the "fishing rights" available to the government to investigate possible antitrust violations prior to an actual case. The 1962 Antitrust Civil Process Act expanded considerably the Antitrust

5. Charles A. Bane, *The Electrical Equipment Conspiracies: The Treble Damage Actions* (New York: Federal Legal Publications, 1973), chaps. 3–5, 7–9.

6. On January 12, 1973, IBM and Control Data Corporation reached an agreement to settle an antitrust suit out of court. In the settlement were several oral understandings, including the agreement that Control Data would destroy all of its attorney work-product relating to the suit. Control Data destroyed a computerized index to 27 million documents as a result of this settlement. The Department of Justice claims that the destruction of the data base "will have the effect, as IBM well knows . . . of impeding the United States in its preparation and trial" of its own suit against IBM. See *Antitrust & Trade Regulation Report* (Washington: Bureau of National Affairs, January 30, 1973).

7. American Bar Association, *Antitrust Developments 1955–1968* (Chicago: American Bar Association, 1968), p. 230, and chap. 8 generally.

Division's ability to gather evidence for an investigation, even prior to the institution of an action, by issuing civil investigative demands. The Federal Trade Commission counterpart, unavailable to private parties, is the section 6(b) report power, which "has now emerged as one of the Commission's most important all-purpose investigatory tools."[8] Court decisions have also given administrative agencies broader subpoena powers to be used at the investigative stage than private plaintiffs have. Finally, in the case of possible criminal violations of the antitrust laws, the Antitrust Division can empanel a grand jury to begin its investigation, and a grand jury has the power to interrogate witnesses under oath without the presence of the witness's lawyer. This option is not open to a private plaintiff. To grant any of these investigatory powers to the private sector would clearly involve enormous potential for abuses.[9]

On balance, the public agency has the edge in investigating antitrust violations, if not in litigating them as well. Casual evidence of this point is manifested by the simple fact that every important development in antitrust law (except those dealing specifically with matters unique to private suits) has occurred in government suits.

The more interesting issue is what effect the absence of private treble damage enforcement would have on the efficacy of public enforcement. The answer to this question hinges on the impact of the elimination of private damage suits would have on private parties' current practice of informing the enforcement agencies about possible antitrust violations. Note that at the present time the agencies rely heavily on such com-

8. Ibid., at p. 220, pp. 243–244.
9. Granting sweeping and far-reaching investigatory powers to private enforcers is not without precedent. Nor is it without historical implications. In the late sixteenth and early seventeenth centuries the grant by the sovereign of monopoly power over certain commodities often included the right for the patentee to enter private dwellings and search the premises and the right to seize "contraband" goods. Eventually, private enforcement was seen as an oppressive encroachment on the rights and dignity of the private citizen and protests were voiced in Parliament. Queen Elizabeth was compelled to admit the abuses and state that grants of patents would no longer be eligible for such violations of common law tradition. See Hans B. Thorelli, *The Federal Antitrust Policy: Origination of an American Tradition* (Baltimore: Johns Hopkins Press, 1955), pp. 25–26.

plaints; in fact, one antitrust official admitted that the agency operated "out of the mailbox."[10]

At first glance, it might seem that without the attraction of potential compensation following a successful government suit, private parties would have no incentive to inform the public agencies of violations observed "in the field." But further thought indicates that the costs of providing such information are so low and the gains (even without compensation) so adequate that such information will continue to flow into the enforcement agencies. Consider a simple example. A firm believes it is buying from a cartel, basing its opinion on a recent price increase by all suppliers or a suspicious pattern in the submission of price bids. At only minimal costs, without even the services of legal counsel, it can write an enforcement agency about its beliefs. The payoffs of doing so, even in the absence of treble damages, are still very real. If the antitrust agency successfully prosecutes the cartel, and the cartel is penalized and deterred by a significant fine, the informer may benefit through lower prices. In fact, the incentives for an informer to provide information about possible antitrust violations may actually be increased in the absence of treble damages because of the concomitant elimination of moral hazard counterincentives.

In short, the difficulty of eliminating private actions is not that of having to rely on a less efficacious or less adequately armed public sector, one that will then encounter serious difficulties gathering information. The more serious question, under a system of fines, is what recourse a private party will have if it believes it is being financially aggrieved by a monopolistic practice but it cannot persuade any government agency to bring a suit? The only recourse is to permit the private party to bring the suit, with relief taking the form of simple injunctive relief rather than damages.

The fourth question that arises concerns possible equity arguments for compensating victims of antitrust violations. Does not a standard of equity or justice demand that parties aggrieved by illegal anticompetitive practices be compensated? The conventional justification for

10. Mark J. Green, et al., *The Closed Enterprise System* (New York: Grossman Publishers, 1972), p. 119.

treble damage suits, after all, is purportedly to compensate the aggrieved victims, not necessarily to provide an efficient deterrent mechanism.[11] The question of equity cannot so readily be divorced from that of efficiency, however. The real question is how much society is willing to give up, in the form of real income, in order to achieve the normative end of perfect equity, that is, full restitution? For as shown earlier, to achieve equity in reparations would involve perverse incentives, the generation of misinformation, and reparations costs.

It should be understood that, given the present state of economic knowledge, the ability to achieve perfect equity does not exist. To make full restitution to all parties injured by anticompetitive practices would require a precise understanding of the incidence of monopolistic distortions. That is, the consumer's surplus lost by each individual buying not only directly from the monopolist but also from all the intermediaries who dealt with the monopolist down to the final consumer would have to be determined. In addition, those customers who find that under monopoly their marginal evaluations of the monopolized product are less than the monopoly price (but equal to or greater than the competitive price) would also require compensation. Moreover, monopoly affects not only the purchasers but also the factors of production as well. Indeed the "exploitation" of the factors of production is considered by Joan Robinson to be the chief disadvantage of monopolistic market structures.[12]

The problem of determining the identity of those damaged by monopoly and the extent of their damages is analogous to the problem of determining the incidence or burden of a tax. Just as a tax drives a wedge between the relative prices faced by the consumer and the producer in the market, so too a monopolist, in charging a price above marginal cost, alters the proportions and relative quantities in which different consumer goods and intermediate products are produced and the proportions and relative quantities in which the services of factors

11. This is the position of Lawrence Vold. See his "Are Threefold Damages Under the Antitrust Act Penal or Compensatory?" *Kentucky Law Journal* 28 (January 1940): 117.

12. Joan Robinson, *The Economics of Imperfect Competition* (London: Macmillan, 1933), chap. 25.

are combined. Few topics in economics have received such sustained attention as the question of who actually bears the burden of various taxes. Yet in spite of these efforts, one authority concluded, relating to the whole question of incidence:

> This . . . question . . . has been the subject of much discussion among businessmen, politicians, and economists for decades, without any satisfactory resolution, even among the experts. In the 1960's several important studies were devoted to this topic, with the result that the average student has become perhaps more confused than he ever was.[13]

These words are highly suggestive. For determining the incidence of who loses wealth because of monopolistic practices would be subject to at least as much difficulty and controversy. Many considerations that might seem extraneous would necessarily have to be brought to bear before there could be an ultimate resolution. Even so remote a consideration as monetary and fiscal policy would have to be analyzed in order to determine the wealth losses of all parties affected. For example, the loss in income sustained by workers following the formation of a cartel would be less if monetary and fiscal policies were aimed at maintaining full employment.[14]

Equity, unlike butterflies, is not free. Even if advances were made in economic science which enabled the full disclosure of all damages resulting from monopoly and the courts were to accept them as relevant, there would still be important costs to society associated with repara-

13. James M. Buchanan, *The Public Finances,* 3d ed. (Homewood, Ill.: Irwin, 1970), p. 264.

14. Without elaborating on the current status of the law on who has been damaged by various antitrust violations (the so-called standing-to-sue issue), it is clear that little attempt is made to fully compensate those who have been injured. In fact, the judicial emphasis excludes consideration of many indirect effects, and, in the case of factors of production, precludes standing to parties immediately affected. Moreover, by eliminating the passing-on defense, even the implications of the simplest partial equilibrium model of incidence are seemingly ignored. See Earl E. Pollock, "Automatic Treble Damages and the Passing-On Defense: The Hanover Shoe Decision," *Antitrust Bulletin* 13 (Winter 1968): 1183.

tions.[15] The misinformation effect would presumably disappear under perfect disclosure. But with damage estimation problems resolved, perverse incentives and reparations costs would remain.

The fifth question requires only brief discussion. The class action suit is unlikely to provide a vehicle for conserving judicial resources by enabling many individual plaintiffs to be joined together in a single lawsuit. While judicial efficiency may have been one of the hopes of the class action device, many observers now see the liberalization of rules permitting class actions as a chief contributor to court congestion.[16] Class action suits, which are frequently multidistrict in nature, involve substantial difficulties in the judicial determination of class members, the disputes over competing class action motions, the problems in the notification of class members (and possible procedures for potential members to opt out), the assignment and coordination of judges in the case of multidistrict litigation, and the impracticalities of notifying and compensating successful, though dispersed, class members. Such problems arise in coordinating and resolving competing claims.

The final question is whether the proposal to eliminate the reparations feature of antitrust law should apply to all torts where injury and compensation are issues. This extension of the proposal might very well apply in torts whenever there are great difficulties in identifying the offense, precisely determining who has been injured, and measuring the extent of the injuries. Where any or all of these determinations are vague or imprecisely defined, tortious actions will involve these inefficiencies. However, torts usually involve actions in which such questions as who has been injured are much clearer than in antitrust cases.

15. It should be noted that in a world where the damages from monopoly can be measured with complete accuracy, monopolists would be unable to pay full damages, much less treble damages, since the welfare loss to consumers from monopoly is always greater than the monopolist's profits. The recommendation of a fine in lieu of reparations for all damages is a recognition of this point because it makes no pretense at exact compensation.

16. For example, Milton Handler concluded there was then "little doubt that massive class actions constitute a net liability for antitrust, for federal courts, and society generally" ("Shift from Substantive to Procedural Innovations in Antitrust Suits—The Twenty-Third Annual Antitrust Review," *Columbia Law Review* 71 [January 1971]: 1).

Quite apart from the disadvantages of private actions suggested by this analysis, there are other reasons for opting for public enforcement of the antitrust laws. These advantages were first suggested by one of the most vigorous and sagacious men to head the Antitrust Division, and consequently one whose advocacy of stringent enforcement cannot be questioned. Thurman Arnold strongly opposed private antitrust suits, only secondarily because he saw them as misdirecting antitrust enforcement, seldom dovetailing with the general consumer interest, and providing a convenient excuse for underfunding government enforcement agencies. Arnold's primary objection was philosophical: he saw private antitrust suits as a type of vigilante justice wholly inappropriate for governing the business sector. He recognized that private enforcement leads to a disrespect for the institutions of law and "can only be justified as a transitory necessity to meet an emergency situation."[17]

17. Thurman Arnold, *The Bottlenecks of Business* (New York: Reynal and Hitchcock, 1940), p. 166.

9

APPLYING OCCAM'S RAZOR

In retrospect it seems remarkable how little emphasis was put on the importance of altering the private actions approach to antitrust enforcement in all of the discussions preceding the final drafting of the Antitrust Procedures and Penalties Act of 1974. The thrust was toward doing more of everything and less of nothing. For example, the original version of the bill introduced by Senator John Tunney provided only a tenfold increase in corporate maximum fines. The crime was to be allowed to remain a misdemeanor rather than a felony because, in the original version, the maximum term for imprisonment was limited to one year. The American Bar Association objected to the original change in penalties only on the grounds that penalizing antitrust violations with high fines (relative to those imposed for actions that are considered felonies, such as arson, forgery, tax evasion, and assaulting the president of the United States) meant that there was a disparity in treatment that raised doubts as to the reasonableness of the increased fine. The ABA concluded that the remedy (later adopted) was not to decrease the proposed fine, but to increase the maximum duration of imprisonment.[1]

The American Bar Association's only exception to the "more of everything" philosophy was in its opposition to any increase in fines on individuals. This reluctance was not based on the inability to identify the actual instigator of the antitrust infraction in a large corporate bureaucracy, but rather on the ABA's opinion that monetary fines do

---

1. *Report to the Council of the Section of Antitrust Law re Proposed "Antitrust Procedures and Penalties Act,"* as cited in U.S., Congress, Senate, Committee on the Judiciary, Subcommittee on Antitrust and Monopoly, *Hearings, The Antitrust Procedures and Penalties Act,* 93d Cong., 1st Sess., 1973, pp. 437–438.

not have the same deterrent effect as imprisonment.[2] Such a view, however, rests on a misunderstanding of the nature of trade-offs between one penalty and another and lacks the economist's insight that every penalty has some monetary equivalent.

The 1974 legislation is the latest manifestation of the continuing American interest in antitrust reform. We hope and predict that this concern will not end with the enactment of these alterations in the penalties, because these changes repeat most of the mistakes of the past. As part I's historical survey of the penalties shows, the American concern with antitrust has too often led to the development of a host of weapons mixed into an amalgam of public and private enforcement. It is tempting to try to do more of everything, to advance on all fronts, when the costs of such a multipronged attack are not understood or recognized. But merely changing an antitrust violation from a misdemeanor to a felony and allowing imprisonment of up to three years does not overcome the practical problems that have historically plagued the jail penalty nor come to grips with the relative inefficiencies of this weapon. Moreover, raising the potential fine to $1 million will not necessarily raise the levies ultimately imposed. Such fines might also fall disproportionately on those least able to afford them and fail to affect significantly those business enterprises most in need of deterrence.

The discussion of the instruments of antitrust policy in part II leads ineluctably to a rather sweeping recommendation for the streamlining of the antitrust tool kit. A severe monetary exaction paid to the state by violators should be the sole instrument of antitrust enforcement. There is some fine capable in principle of being as effective as *any* other instrument of deterrence; in terms of additional scarce resources the cost of such a fine (once a violation has been detected and convicted) is in fact zero. And no other instrument requires so few and such simple bureaucratic channels to implement. The advantages of the fine are clear and compelling. The inefficiencies associated with the perverse incentives and misinformation effects would be eliminated; the judicial and economic difficulties arising from the draconian pen-

2. Ibid., p. 425.

alty that consigns businessmen to jail would be bypassed; and the additional scarce resources inevitably used up in the laudable but vain attempt to assess damages and recompense injured parties would be salvaged for alternative and more highly productive uses. Indeed this weapon should appeal most agreeably to economists who have taken the traditional view of the monopoly problem. It is the only instrument that can justify on economic grounds a completely vigorous and single-minded antitrust policy, for no other weapon is consistent with an attempt to bring about conditions approximating perfect competition.

The case for increasing financial penalties as an alternative to increasing the volume of resources flowing into increased detection and conviction of antitrust violators is even stronger when the risk attitudes of American management are considered.

Furthermore, the use of a single high financial penalty in the corporate world of risk aversion could provide incentives for enforcing any antitrust results that are deemed appropriate, whether in the form of structure, conduct, or performance benchmarks. As has been stated from first page to last, this book has not been concerned with the issue of which standards ought to prevail, but with efficient deterrence of antitrust violations, however construed. The proposal of a high financial exaction should appeal to antitrust proponents of any persuasion. For example, those who believe that the deconcentration of industry is the route to competitive behavior would surely applaud a high monetary toll that would lead a firm to take steps to lower its market share until the firm is well within the bounds of legality.[3] Adherents of a strong antimerger program would find that businesses would have a prudent regard for the antitrust agencies' guidelines when considering acquisitions, because any firms that violated the law would be subject to the fine until the merger was undone. If rigid and inflexible pricing behavior is considered to be the genuine defect of oligopolistic market structures, a fine could be levied that would

3. A plan for reducing the government's and the court's involvement in the mechanics of divestiture has been outlined in an ingenious suggestion by William L. Baldwin. See "Selective Divestiture By Spin-Off and Lottery: A Modest Proposal," *Antitrust Law & Economics Review* 6 (Winter 1972–73): 107.

induce oligopolists to avoid even tacit collusion. Prohibiting such business practices as tying contracts, if they were considered to be inefficient, would be accomplished automatically under threat of severe financial pain.

Almost every student of antitrust, whether in law or economics, encounters at the outset the famous case of *Darcy* v. *Allen,* a private action against monopoly brought under the English common law.[4] The introductory student learns how this private suit ended the playing card monopoly in England and weakened the crown's prerogative to grant monopoly franchises. In recommending a significant reversal of the present trend of private antitrust enforcement, it would be idle to contend that there are no instances where private damage actions today do not yield socially beneficial results of the *Darcy* v. *Allen* nature. Moreover, there is no doubt that institutional modifications could be attempted that would move in the direction of alleviating some of the grosser inefficiencies now found under current treble damage provisions. For example, allowing the defense of *in pari delicto* and contributory negligence, the assignment of defendant's legal fees (and all other costs) to unsuccessful plaintiffs, a clarification of what constitutes an antitrust offense, and other such reforms discussed earlier would give lesser scope to these inefficiencies. Unfortunately, the latest antitrust reforms do not in any way come to grips with them.

In contrast to a multipronged attempt to improve the private damage suit, we have suggested a simpler proposal for deterring monopolistic behavior: an optimal fine without compensation. This proposal squares with the public goods nature of antitrust enforcement and recognizes the reciprocal nature of monopoly damages. It also bypasses the enormous difficulties in equitably compensating injured parties and dovetails with recent developments in welfare economics that question compensation itself on efficiency grounds.[5] Moreover, the costs stemming from perverse incentives and misinformation ef-

---

4. *Darcy* v. *Allen* (The Case of Monopolies), 77 Eng. Rep. 1260, 11 Co. Rep. 846 (1602).

5. William J. Baumol, "On Taxation and the Control of Externalities," *American Economic Review* 62 (June 1972): 307, 313.

fects would be obviated and reparations costs excised. Thus a fine could accomplish skillfully and adroitly what a host of instruments could achieve at best only imperfectly. Such pruning is imperative if our antitrust penalties are to bear the full fruit of their potential.

INDEX

Adams, Henry Carter, 24
Adams, Walter, 46
Administrative Office of the United States Courts, 141
Alcoa case, x, 51
Alioto, Joseph, 75
American Bar Association, 58, 75, 149
American Can Co. v. *Russellville Canning Co.,* 86, 89
American Sugar Refining Co., 18*n*
American Tobacco case, 28, 45, 51
Antitrust: enforcement, 7–16; increase in suits, 12*n*, proposed amendments to laws, 33, 38, 39, 40, 56, 58, 59, 60, 61 64–65; English statutes, 63, 64
Antitrust Civil Process Act (*1972*), 142–43
Antitrust Division, 11, 15, 115, 119, 139, 142, 143
Antitrust League, 25
Antitrust Procedures and Penalties Act (*1974*), ix, 42, 61, 141*n*, 149
Arnall, Ellis, 118–19
Arnold, Thurman, 148
Atlas Building Products Co. v. *Diamond Block & Gravel Co.,* 70*n*
Attorney General's National Committee to Study the Antitrust Laws, 65, 84

Ball, Thomas, 19
Bane, Charles, 87
Beall, Jack, 25

Becker, Gary S., 116
Bigelow v. *RKO Radio Pictures, Inc.,* 70*n*, 93*n*
Black, Hugo, 89
Blatz Brewing Co., 53
Blaylock, Arvel, 86–87
Bluefields S.S. Co. v. *United Fruit Co.,* 89*n*
Brandeis, Louis, 22, 45
Breckenridge, William, 21
Brown Shoe Co. v. *U.S.,* 44*n*
Buchanan, James M., 146
Bureau of Corporations, 23
Burton, John F., 32, 56

Celler-Kefauver Act, 46
Census Bureau, 11*n*, 107–08
Chamberlin, Edward H., 8, 107
Chicago Conference on Trusts (*1907*), 29, 65
Chilton, Horace, 33
Clabault, James M., 32, 56
Clark, J. M., 7–9
Clark, John D., 67
Class action suits, 14, 71, 73*n*, 75, 95, 139, 147
Clayton Act: passage of, 29; and imprisonment, 31*n*, 40; and structural relief, 46–47, 52–53; and fines, 60; and treble damages, 63*n*; and private enforcement, 68, 69; and attorneys' fees, 72; and misinformation effect, 95*n*
"Clean hands," 71, 89*n*